EXPERIMENTS IN
GOTHIC STRUCTURE

The MIT Press
Cambridge, Massachusetts
London, England

EXPERIMENTS IN
GOTHIC STRUCTURE

Robert Mark

Publication of this volume has been aided by
a grant from the National Endowment for the
Humanities.

Photographs without a credit line were taken
by Robert Mark.

This book was set in Trump Mediæval by
Village Typographers, Inc. Color plates printed
by Mark-Burton Inc. Printed and bound by
Halliday Lithograph in the United States
of America.

Library of Congress Cataloging in Publication
Data

Mark, Robert.
    Experiments in Gothic structure.

    Bibliography: p.
    Includes index.
    1. Architecture, Gothic. I. Title.
NA440.M36   723'.5   82–25
ISBN 0–262–13170–6   AACR2

From the moment that flying buttresses became
sharply defined in buildings, the development
of church structure . . . set out boldly in a
new direction. To ask for a Gothic church without flying buttresses is to ask for a ship without
a keel; for church as for ship, it is a question
of being or not being.

E. E. Viollet-le-Duc (1854)

CONTENTS

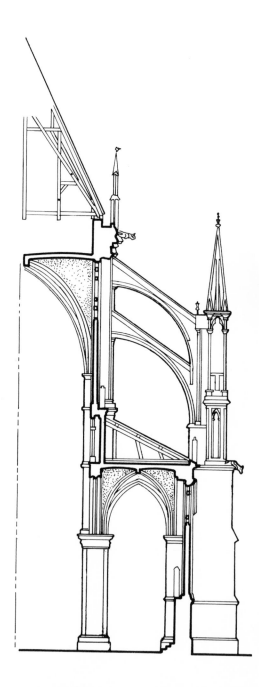

PREFACE

During my college years I went to an interview for an engineering job carrying under my arm Sabartes's *Picasso* with its brightly colored jacket. The interview was unsuccessful. Later, as I waited for an elevator in the corridor, one of the engineers, apparently feeling sympathetic, emerged from his office to give advice: "Young man, never bring a book like *that* when you look for a job in engineering." This dichotomy in my interests continued until some fifteen years ago when several architecture students who were taking a course on medieval architecture in addition to my course on structures pointed to the dearth of scientific analysis of Gothic cathedral structure.

The technology underlying all works of architecture, and particularly monumental structures, is frequently too complex to be readily grasped by most observers or even by the authors of influential architectural treatises, who often overlook or misinterpret important technical elements. Architectural historians readily acknowledge that the history of architecture is the study of both art and building technology, yet their training is rarely adequate to allow them to perform definitive technical analysis. In fact, it is only relatively recently that engineers themselves have developed analysis techniques that can cope with many of the questions raised about structural design and performance— probably the most enigmatic aspect of the technology of historic buildings. These techniques may involve the analysis of a small-scale physical model of a structure under scaled loadings or the setting out in an electronic computer of a mathematical description of the geometric form of a building structure and the behavior of its materials.

Small-scale models are widely used by architects today both to study relationships between the components of a building and to convey design ideas to a client. Although not directly mentioned in early manuscripts, the same technique may well have been used in the medieval era. It is also possible that certain types of models were used to work out construction details, and it is even conceivable, if unlikely, that scaled models, assembled stone by stone, were used to test for the overall stability of new architectural forms. Yet even this type of model could not have adequately predicted the structural behavior of a full-scale building under the action of all natural forces. Such predictions only became possible when modern engineers developed reliable, accurate techniques to measure model response (shown by displacements, strains, and stresses) and established the dimensional analysis criteria that related this response to a full-scale prototype. In addition, numerical computer modeling, which has developed into an almost routine engineering tool in the last decade, can now accomplish much the same task as investigations based on physical models.

The use of both technical approaches has resulted in a greatly improved understanding of the structural role of the elements of a number of historic buildings. The studies of the large medieval churches described in this text have been particularly enlightening because hitherto the intricacy of church structure has thwarted accurate perception of structural function. Even regions of the masonry construction that were by no means obvious candidates for distress were pinpointed and later confirmed when I had an opportunity to visit the buildings and observe that special attention for these specific regions was indeed required from the maintenance staffs.

The impetus to publish a summary of the investigations derived from a seminar on "Structure and Gothic Architecture" that I gave at Princeton with the art historian Carolyn Malone. Preparing for the seminar led me to review and reinterpret both my own views and those of other writers. Additional incentive came from the knowledge that colleagues in other institutions were, for lack of a single comprehensive publication, assigning reprints of our papers in their courses on the history of architecture and on technical history. And these reprints are not always easy to find because the spectrum of interest in this research is so broad—ranging from art history to engineering—that articles on the specific investigations have appeared in a very wide range of journals, including *American Scientist, Annals of the New York Academy of Science, Art Bulletin, Experimental Mechanics, Journal of the Society of Architectural Historians, Scientific American, Speculum, Transactions of the New York Academy of Science,* and *Technology and Culture.* (Specific publications on which material in the text is based are cited with the notes of each chapter.) A negative result of this diversity has been that no scholar can follow the thread of the work from publications in any single field, and few libraries contain the complete series. Finally, juxtaposition of the major studies clarifies trends in design that evolved throughout the era.

The text is aimed at the general reader as well as the student of Gothic architecture. The technical approach is described in chapter 2, and further details and definitions are included in an appendix. These descriptions are relatively simple, with the sources of more detailed information on the buildings and the analysis techniques either given, or referred to, in notes. A dual system of units (metric and English) is generally used; for clarity, certain drawings display only a single unit system.

As with any truly interdisciplinary research, important contributions to the work reported here have been made by specialists across several fields. I am deeply indebted to a number of present and former colleagues at Princeton, particularly to John F. Abel, David P. Billington, and Ahmet Cakmak in engineering; Alan Borg, François Bucher, and the late Donald Drew Egbert in art and architectural history; and to other scholars, including Peter Collins of McGill University, Mary Dean

of the University of Maryland, Harold
Dorn of Stevens Institute of Technology,
Lon R. Shelby of Southern Illinois University, Arnold Wolf, Dombaumeister of
Cologne Cathedral, and Lynn White, Jr.,
professor emeritus of the University of
California, Los Angeles. Many former
students in engineering and architecture
took part in the research, including some
with whom I have collaborated in publication—Kirk Alexander, Ronald Jonash,
Kevin O'Neill, Richard Prentke, and
Maury Wolfe. For several years preceding
his untimely death in 1973, Robert
Branner, medieval art historian at Colum-
bia University, made vital contributions,
particularly to my understanding of the
cathedrals of Bourges and Beauvais.

I wish to express my gratitude also to
the National Endowment for the Humanities, which, together with the Ford and
Rockefeller foundations, sponsored
the program "Humanistic Studies in
Engineering" from 1969 to 1975, of which
this research was a part. I would also like
to thank the National Endowment for
the Humanities, together with the An-
drew W. Mellon Foundation, for sponsoring
an interinstitutional program, "Architecture and the Scientific Revolution," between Princeton and Stevens Institute of
Technology from 1975 to 1979. I am especially indebted to the Endowment for a
Senior Fellowship in 1973–1974, which
enabled me to become familiar with and
to photograph the fabric of the buildings that are the subject of this work.

Finally, I am most grateful to the readers
of the MIT Press and to the following in-
dividuals for their generous assistance:
David P. Billington and Joan Hart for
editorial suggestions, Robert Vuyosevich
for many of the line drawings, and particularly to Yoma Ullman, whose deft
editing has brought order to the text.

EXPERIMENTS IN GOTHIC STRUCTURE

I
THE ENIGMA OF
GOTHIC STRUCTURE

Gothic architecture developed in northern France in the middle of the twelfth century and spread rapidly throughout all of Europe. The vitality of the Gothic is generally attributed to its acceptance as a *style* of building, as distinct, for example, from the Roman style. Yet it also represented a radical new approach to building technology, achieving lightweight, spacious, tall construction in stone.

To emphasize this technological achievement is not to belittle the religious and aesthetic motivations of the Gothic builders. Nevertheless, Hans Jantzen's warning that one can never really understand the construction of that era, since "an insuperable barrier separates their approach to building from ours" is unacceptable.[1] For Jantzen, as well as for many other art historians, this barrier is illustrated by the chronicles of the era that "tell us of the spirit in which the cathedrals were built. . . . 'Lords and princes, full of riches and honours, even women of noble birth, their proud heads bowed, harnessed like beasts of burden to carts, [brought] wine, corn, oil, lime, stones, timbers and other things needful for sustaining life or the fabric of the churches.'"[2]

Although ceremonial pilgrimages corresponding to this description of the cult of carts certainly took place from time to time, such dedication was not enough to bring about the successful construction of the great Gothic churches, which could have been accomplished only by a highly organized crew of artisans. Indeed, historians who have painstakingly sorted out surviving fragments of the building records have recreated an image of the Gothic builders that differs strikingly from Jantzen's description. These builders appear to have worked in relatively well paid, mobile, highly skilled teams of masons and carpenters, with supporting staffs that included the apprentices who ensured the continuity of their skills. The medieval historian, Lynn White, has even observed that "these structures are the first vast monuments in all history to be built by free—nay, unionized—labor."[3]

The supposition that major building projects and, in particular, new technical innovations, were developed by a nucleus of hired professionals is given further credibility by the economic and social conditions of the time. The expansion of trade and the rise of marketing and manufacturing centers in the twelfth century brought about unprecedented changes in western European society. With the growth of medieval cities, these changes included the appearance of new economic and social classes: first, the commercial middle class, and later, the specialized industrial proletariat.[4]

The monetary basis of medieval trade and capitalism, which fueled this movement from the mid-twelfth century on, owed a great deal to the circulation of liquid capital, which in turn was an outgrowth of the early crusades. Feudal, clerical, and royal crusaders mortgaged and sold their fixed holdings to obtain cash to buy equipment, hire soldiers, and pay passage to the East.[5] Much of this liquid capital, reinvested for profit in European commerce, found its way through donations by wealthy merchants into the numerous large-scale church building campaigns begun in the major towns near the end of the twelfth century. Indeed, High Gothic architecture was itself a phenomenon of urban growth. Mercantile and ecclesiastical centers vied with each other over the height of their buildings, as Chicago and New York were to do seven centuries later.[6]

Contemporaneous records of medieval design and construction techniques are almost nonexistent.[7] Yet we do have access to one important document, the sketchbook of Villard de Honnecourt, which dates from the thirteenth century, and it is also possible to extrapolate certain information from later fifteenth-century Gothic design booklets.[8]

Villard de Honnecourt's sketchbook contains plans and views of major buildings of his time along with a number of sketches and some slight text dealing with such topics as the setting out and the cutting of stone, timber roof and floor details, machines including a water-powered saw mill and a screw jack, and applied geometry. But Villard provides no clues about the construction sequence or about what is possibly the most crucial aspect of masonry construction: the extensive timber centering that provided support for both workmen and stonework during the course of erection.[9] We do know, however, that the timber roof across the main arcade was generally placed prior to the erection of the high vaults so that the roof framing was employed as part of a lifting system to raise the materials needed to construct the vaults.

Models and drawings used for design have survived only from the late Middle Ages.[10] Medieval design techniques seem to have been almost wholly concerned with inscribing geometric figures—circles, squares, triangles, and octagons—to compose the configuration of architectural elements. A number of medieval tracing floors have been discovered, sometimes on lead or stone surfaces over side aisle roofs, where geometric compositions were carried out at full scale. Surviving fragments of building accounts indicate that the medieval mason was unfamiliar even with simple multiplication, which explains the prevalance of geometry in design rather than any form of arithmetic computation. Villard himself demonstrates extensive use of geometry in such matters as shaping the keystone of an arch or measuring the height of a tower from ground observations using similar triangles.

There is, however, no reference in Villard, or for that matter in any of the notebooks prior to the end of the fifteenth century, to any rules that might ensure sound structure. And even the much later rules are entirely empirical.[11] The beginnings of modern analytical structural theory in Galileo's seminal *Two New Sciences* were still a century off.

Despite the limitations in design technique, development of new structural systems during the course of the twelfth century was prodigious. The evolution in building form that led to High Gothic architecture can be illustrated by a comparison of three major buildings whose construction dates span the epoch: Sainte-Foy at Conques, a Romanesque, rural pilgrimage church begun around 1050 and largely completed in the first quarter of the twelfth century (figures 1a, 2, and 3), the early Gothic cathedral of Laon, begun around 1160 and completed by about 1215 (figures 1b and 4), and the classic High Gothic cathedral of Reims, begun in 1211 and remaining in various phases of construction for some 80 years (figures 1c, 5, and 6).

Notwithstanding its considerable height—21 m (69 ft) to the keystones of its vaults—and the fairly wide openings along the arcade, the interior of Sainte-Foy (figure 3) presents an almost tunnel-like quality compared with the light, open stone frame of the considerably taller Reims Cathedral or even with Laon Cathedral, which is not significantly higher than Sainte-Foy at 24 m (79 ft). The cross section of Sainte-Foy (figure 1a) reveals that the vertical weight and the outward thrust from the barrel vaulting are carried by the heavy piers, which in turn are laterally braced at the point of attachment to the vault by transverse walls above the side aisle galleries. Light enters the upper region of the church through small windows at the perimeter of the building so that the central aisle is only indirectly lighted.

At Laon the raised clerestory, integrated with the ribbed vaulting, has large windows that admit far more light to the interior of the building (figure 4). This achievement derives from a wall structure of greater intricacy. More developed transverse walls abutting the triforium above the side aisle galleries provide the necessary lateral support to the clerestory wall (figure 1b).

At Reims the lofty clerestory wall, embellished with stained glass in enlarged openings (figures 5 and 6), is the apotheosis of the Gothic ideal, which aimed for a display of daring structure admitting the maximum amount of light.[12] The principal features of its structure included quadripartite, pointed, ribbed vaults supported at regular intervals on tall piers and their extensions, which were themselves supported laterally at the level of the clerestory by tiers of flying buttresses. Load-bearing exterior walls were not required, and their place was largely taken by windows. The height of the central aisle of this building is striking: 38 m (124 ft) from the floor to the keystone of the highest vault, the height of a twelve-story building. A high-peaked, timber roof, supported on raised parapets above the clerestory, then adds another 22 m (72 ft) to the building's overall height.

The attainment of this ideal in very tall churches, however, posed certain crucial problems. The first was economic. As the buildings grew larger, the cost—which must have appeared to be almost insupportable—of obtaining and transporting vast amounts of stone, often from distant quarries, and of shaping the individual stones and setting them into place, demanded more economical design.[13] The second problem concerned structural forces. The higher superstructures, in addition to having to resist the outward thrust of the interior vaulting, were subject to great wind forces, as were the high wooden roofs above them. Transverse walls above the side aisles, which had hitherto provided sufficient bracing against these lateral forces, were inadequate to the new demands. A third consideration was the need to reduce the weight of the superstructure in order to relieve the footings under the piers and thereby allay their settlement.

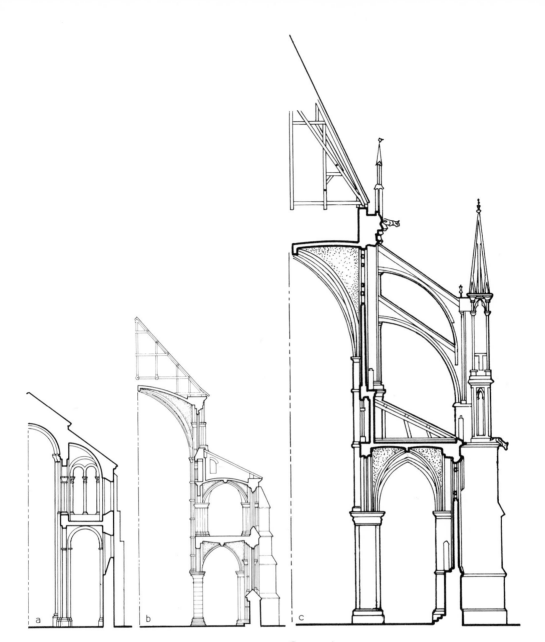

1 Comparative cross
sections through the
naves of (a) Sainte-Foy,
Conques, begun ca. 1050;
(b) Laon Cathedral, be-
gun ca. 1160; (c) Reims
Cathedral, begun 1211.

2 Sainte-Foy, Conques.
View from the northeast.

3 Sainte-Foy, Conques.
Interior as seen from the
nave.

4 Laon Cathedral. Interior seen from the nave. Photo by W. Clark.

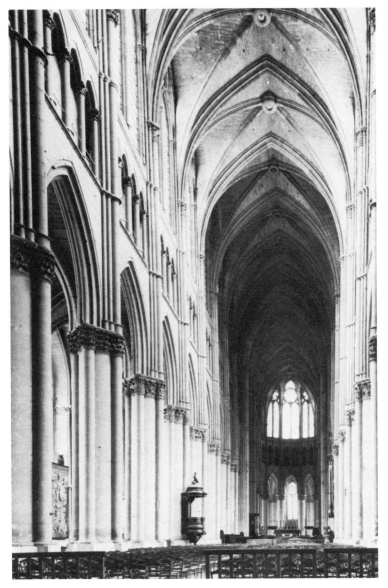

5 Reims Cathedral.
Interior of the nave.

6 Reims Cathedral. Flying
buttress supporting the
nave clerestory.

The combination of these factors led to the invention of the exposed flying buttress, which extended between the outer clerestory wall and the pier buttress above the side aisle roof (figure 1c). This new device allowed the lightening of the clerestory structure while effectively supporting it. For the history of art, though, its most important effect was to redefine the style of Gothic churches.

It has been generally accepted that the first true flying buttresses were used shortly before 1180, in the tallest building of the twelfth century, Notre Dame in Paris, to provide stability to the clerestory above the nave.[14] By the turn of the twelfth century, the full potential of the new development was realized at the cathedrals of Chartres and Bourges, enabling the clerestory wall to be reduced to a skeletal frame enclosing large areas of glass.

Three categories of questions have been raised about Gothic design. The first concerns the mystery of how so remarkable a technical achievement was brought about given the dearth of scientific methodology. The second concerns nineteenth-century attitudes toward Gothic structural form and function that have become deeply embedded in twentieth-century architectural theory. This has occurred because the structure of Gothic buildings is so complex that speculation about structural function is often based on a particular writer's bias with respect to technology vis-à-vis art. Opinions range from those of the so-called rationalists, who view all the elements of the Gothic cathedral as the result of optimum design rather than of fashion, to those of the antirational illusionists, who are appalled by the idea that great beauty could arise primarily from structural considerations and would prefer to think that fashion also played a major role in the development of those elements. The third category of questions concerns present-day architecture: how does our knowledge of the functioning of Gothic structure help to explain the viability of certain elements of modern architecture?

The questions raised by the first category may be answered in part by considering the iterative nature of modern structural design. In almost all cases, a designer first selects a particular form from several practicable solutions; for example, to span a long space he may choose a system of girders, trusses, or arches. This selection is primarily based on past experience in design and the economics of construction and, usually to a lesser extent, on analytical knowledge. In the second step of the design process, the form is analyzed to determine its performance, usually by hand computation, possibly assisted by the use of a structural model, or, more frequently today, by an electronic computer. To improve the safety of the design, its economy (usually by reducing the amount of material required), or its performance (for example, by reducing unwanted deflection), yet a third step of redesign to refine the original form often follows. A fourth step then repeats the analysis in step two, which may then entail still another redesign, and so on until the designer is satisfied that no further refinement is called for. For certain critical structures that must be highly refined, such as bridges with very long spans, the last stage of analysis entails testing the completed structure with instruments to observe its behavior under actual loads.

When the great Gothic churches were built, and indeed until nineteenth-century industrial development and its introduction of new construction materials brought the more common use of the science of mechanics into structural analysis, the design process was, of course, different. Nevertheless, the first and most important step of the process—design based on previous experience—was virtually the same. And the system of apprenticeship ensured that medieval designers were familiar with earlier design and construction techniques. The progression of design over a period of about a century and a half, with its implicit suggestion of improvement through accumulated experience, is illustrated by the building sections shown in figure 1, which make it clear that High Gothic form, as exemplified by Reims, did not come into being overnight. Certain Gothic design elements, such as ribbed vaults, began to appear at the turn of the eleventh century, and others, such as the increasingly diaphanous structure of walls, continued to develop throughout the twelfth century.

The second step of the prescientific design process might have used a small-scale model, constructed similarly to the full-scale prototype, to test the design for gross stability or, in other words, to test the resistance of the structure against overturning or rotating to destruction under the action of gravity. Such a model, however, could not have been used to predict the strength of the actual building.[15] Hence the second step of this early design process probably involved the construction of the building itself at full scale—in effect, paralleling the last testing stage of modern analysis by observing performance under actual loading.

This course was not as perilous as it might appear, since the facts of structural behavior, even if not fully grasped by medieval builders, mitigated some of the problems that could be encountered in the full-scale building. In the first place, the form and method of construction of each new building retained many of the elements from earlier designs. In effect, therefore, an earlier building often acted as an approximate model that would confirm the stability of the new one. The second mitigating factor was that the buildings were often constructed by raising the superstructure of one bay at a time. Hence only the first bays would require reconstruction if design problems became evident. Finally, the strength of masonry in compression rarely governs structural failure, since it is far greater than the strength of masonry in tension. Instead it is considerations of gross stability and the absence or presence of tension within the weak mortar between stones that usually determine whether a masonry building

is sound. The crucial role of such tension explains why the studies of medieval churches by means of models discussed in this text are concerned mainly with locating and assessing possible regions in the buildings where tension might occur.

The central character in the second category of questions, which concerns the issue of technology versus art in Gothic architecture, is Eugène Emmanuel Viollet-le-Duc (1814–1879), architect, restorer, and prolific author of treatises on the techniques and interpretation of historic architecture. As a result of his experience as principal architect in charge of the restoration of a number of French Gothic cathedrals, including Amiens, Chartres, Reims, and Notre Dame in Paris (figure 7 shows a statue of him above the crossing), Viollet-le-Duc became the foremost authority of his time on French medieval construction.

Unlike many of his contemporaries, who advocated the wholesale revival of the Gothic style for nineteenth-century architecture, Viollet-le-Duc examined historic buildings with the goal of deducing from them general principles whose modern application might lead to new, rational architecture. He perceived the Gothic style as the product of a secular intellectual movement and persuasively argued that many of the style's principal elements, especially the flying buttress, pinnacle, and vault rib, were originally derived from the demands of construction or structural stability. The laws of structural mechanics, Viollet-le-Duc proclaimed, apply to all architecture at all times, and it is the response to these laws with appropriate structural design that creates true style: "We have various opinions respecting the method of expressing our ideas in architecture . . . but we are all agreed as to the rules dictated by good sense and experience and by the inexorable laws of statics . . . it is not so much the forms of art that we must teach our youth as these invariable principles."[16]

7 Statue of Viollet-le-Duc
above the crossing at
Notre Dame in Paris.

Viollet-le-Duc attempted to demonstrate how the appropriate employment of the new materials of his age, particularly iron, might bring about new styles of architecture. His illustrated designs showing iron architectural elements were awkward in appearance and hence not very convincing. Yet his writings on structural rationalism had vast influence on a whole generation of architects. Indeed he has even been credited with originating the idea of the American skyscraper.[17]

Because his hypothesis took on great importance as a tenet of modern architecture, Viollet-le-Duc's work became the target of considerable controversy among architectural historians.[18] His restorations were criticized as being insensitive to particular periods of medieval construction, and it was pointed out that his own designs, which were few, did not live up to the expectations aroused by his theory. But the strongest criticism came from writers, such as Pol Abraham (1891–1966), who argued that if Viollet-le-Duc's technical analysis of the Gothic was incorrect, then so was the whole concept of structural rationalism. Abraham accused Viollet-le-Duc of employing romanticized mechanics as a substitute for analytic structural mechanics to prop up a subjective thesis;[19] and in the light of Abraham's more modern analysis, inconsistencies in Viollet-le-Duc's reasoning indeed became apparent. But Abraham, trained as an architect, also had difficulties with technical analysis and the result has been a continuing lively debate.

The noted medieval art historian, Paul Frankl, recognizing that his colleagues were not properly trained to settle the matter, urged them in 1960 to collect information on Gothic structure and pass it on to the physicists for help in its interpretation.[20] Actually his appeal to the physicists was at least a half-century too late. Modern physics had veered away from the study of analytic structural mechanics, leaving its development in the hands of research engineers.

The third category of questions concerning the rationale for certain structural elements used in both contemporary and Gothic architecture is closely tied to the question of Gothic rationalism. Despite arguments from Viollet-le-Duc's detractors that flying buttresses are actually ornamental, the logic of the flying buttress in supporting the light, high clerestory walls of High Gothic cathedrals is overwhelming. No one of sound mind would suggest that the flyers be removed from Reims Cathedral, nor would it be propitious to remove them from Pier Luigi Nervi's Small Sports Palace in Rome (figures 8 and 9). The logic of employing diagonal ribs arrayed in a similar fashion to those of a Gothic vault to help to support a groined, thin-shell, concrete roof for the airport at St. Louis, Missouri (figure 10), however, is not at all obvious because of the far greater complexity of its three-dimensional shell structure. Nevertheless, the detailed analysis of Gothic ribbed vaulting described in chapter 8 also provided a means to analyze the airport roof and, in so doing, served to reevaluate Viollet-le-Duc's theory.

This analysis would not have been possible without the experimental and computer modeling techniques that have become available only in recent decades. Structural studies of Gothic buildings that have made use of these powerful new tools have already afforded fresh perceptions and may finally lay to rest much of the controversy concerning rationalism in the context of Gothic architecture.

8 P. L. Nervi, Small Sports
Palace, Rome, 1957.
Thirty-six flying but-
tresses are arranged about
the perimeter.

9 P. L. Nervi, Small Sports
Palace, Rome, 1957.
Interior. The concrete
ribbed roof is composed
of nearly 1,600 precast
elements.

10 Yamasaki, Hellmuth
and Leinweber, airport
terminal, St. Louis, 1955.
The thin concrete shell
roof is composed of
intersecting circular cyl-
inders. Photo by Roberts
and Schaefer Co.

NOTES

For an introduction to Gothic architecture and its precursors, see Robert Branner, *Gothic Architecture* (see note 14), and Whitney S. Stoddard, *Monastery and Cathedral in France* (Middletown, Conn.: Wesleyan University Press, 1966).

1 Hans Jantzen, *High Gothic: The Classic Cathedrals of Chartres, Reims, and Amiens* (New York: Minerva Press, 1962), p. viii.

2 Jantzen, *High Gothic*, p. viii. The quotation is taken from a letter of Abbot Haimon of St. Pierre-sur-Dives in Normandy.

3 Lynn White, Jr., *Dynamo and Virgin Reconsidered* (Cambridge: MIT Press, 1968), p. 63.

4 Hilmar C. Krueger, "Economic Aspects of Expanding Europe," in *Twelfth-Century Europe and the Foundations of Modern Society*, edited by Marshall Clagett, Gaines Post, and Robert Reynolds (Madison: University of Wisconsin Press, 1966), pp. 59–76.

5 Krueger, "Economic Aspects of Expanding Europe," p. 72.

6 See Henri Pirenne, *Medieval Cities, Their Origins and the Revival of Trade* (Princeton: Princeton University Press, 1925), pp. 210ff.

7 Details of medieval construction have been brought to light mainly through modern restoration. Viollet-le-Duc's *Dictionnaire raisonné de l'architecture française du XIe au XVIe siècle*, 10 vols. (Paris: Librairies-Imprimeries Réunies, 1854–1868), particularly the fourth volume, on construction, remains a major source, as does Robert Willis's article on vaulting, "On the Construction of the Vaults of the Middle Ages," *Transactions of the Royal Institute of British Architects of London* I, Part ii (1842):1–69. For medieval timber construction, see C. A. Hewett, *English Cathedral Carpentry* (London: Weyland, 1974).

8 Robert Willis, *Facsimile of the Sketch Book of Wilars de Honecort* (London: Henry & Parker, 1893). For interpretation of fifteenth-century design booklets, see Lon R. Shelby, *Gothic Design Techniques* (Carbondale, Ill.: Southern Illinois University Press, 1977).

9 See John Fitchen, *The Construction of Gothic Cathedrals* (Oxford: Clarendon Press, 1961).

10 See, for example, François Bucher, "Medieval Architectural Design Methods, 800–1560," *Gesta* 11 (1972):37–51. In masonry construction going back to the Roman era, I have observed that while the general configuration of a structure was apparently fixed at an early stage of the project, there was great variation in the shapes of individual stones. Yet this does not suggest the absence of an overall design scheme, as implied by John James, who concludes that "in our sense of the word, there were no architects at all—only building contractors . . . who moved around the countryside from job to job working for as long as the money lasted" (*Chartres les constructeurs* [Chartres: Société Archéologique d'Eure-et-Loir, 1977], p. 1).

11 The booklet of "Instructions" written in 1516 by Lorenz Lechler contains rules for structural proportion. See Lon R. Shelby and Robert Mark, "Late Gothic Structural Design in the 'Instructions' of Lorenz Lechler," *Architectura* 9 (1979):113–131.

12 For a discussion of the affinity of luminosity and the metaphysics of the era, see Otto von Simson, *The Gothic Cathedral*, 2nd ed. (New York: Harper and Row, 1962), pp. 50–58. A scientific view of the effect of architectural scale in relation to light within medieval churches is developed by Stephen Jay Gould in *Ever Since Darwin: Reflections in Natural History* (New York: Norton, 1977), pp. 175–177.

13 The true cost of High Gothic construction can only be surmised from accounts of the cost of stone building in the later Middle Ages, such as those given by Douglas Knoop and G. P. Jones, *The Medieval Mason*, 3rd ed. (New York: Barnes & Noble, 1967).

14 Robert Branner, *Gothic Architecture* (New York: Braziller, 1961), p. 27.

15 See "Modeling Similitude" in appendix.

16 Eugène E. Viollet-le-Duc, *Discourses on Architecture*, 2 vols., translated by Henry Van Brunt (Boston: J. R. Osgood and Co., 1875; originally published in Paris by A. Morel as *Entretiens sur l'architecture*, vol. I in 1863 and vol. II in 1872), II, pp. 144ff.

17 For one example of Viollet-le-Duc's influence, see Donald Hoffman, "Frank Lloyd Wright and Viollet-le-Duc," *Journal of the Society of Architectural Historians* XXVIII (1969):173–184. Sigfried Giedion notes that the Minneapolis architect, Leroy S. Buffington, "claims to have invented the skyscraper in 1880, deriving his inspiration from Viollet-le-Duc's *Discourses*. . . . The passage that aroused his interest occurs in Volume II of the *Discourses* on pages 1–2, where Viollet-le-Duc remarks that a 'practical architect might not unnaturally conceive the idea of erecting a vast edifice whose frame should be entirely of iron, . . . preserving [that frame] by means of a casing of stone'" (*Space, Time and Architecture*, 5th ed., Cambridge: Harvard University Press, 1967, p. 206).

18 For background on the rationalist controversy, see Paul Frankl, *The Gothic: Literary Sources and Interpretations Through Eight Centuries* (Princeton: Princeton University Press, 1960), pp. 799ff.

19 Pol Abraham, *Viollet-le-Duc et le Rationalisme Médiéval* (Paris: Vincent, Fréal & Cie., 1934), p. 102.

20 Frankl, *The Gothic*, p. 810.

2
MODELING GOTHIC STRUCTURE

Modeling theory, including descriptions of the engineering assumptions that underlie it, scaling laws, and the environmental loadings—dead weight and wind—that influenced the form taken by the large Gothic churches, is developed in this chapter. Also included is a brief account of the photoelastic method, as most of the investigations to be discussed are based on the use of this modeling technique. But it should be stressed that the modeling theory applies equally well to other techniques of analysis, including the numerical computer models.[1]

MEDIEVAL MASONRY

In modeling medieval masonry buildings it is necessary to consider the characteristics of the building materials available in the Middle Ages. Granite, limestone, and sandstone were commonly used. Limestone, however, because of its general availability, good qualities of endurance, and relatively easy workability, was most often used for load-bearing walls and piers. The strength of all stone in compression, but particularly of limestone, is quite variable. It is sensitive to such factors as the relationship between the stone's orientation in its natural bed (in situ) and the direction in which forces are applied to it in a building. The compressive strength of limestone ranges from a low of about 200 kg/cm^2 (2,800 psi) to a high of 2,000 kg/cm^2 (28,000 psi). The range of tensile strengths for all stone is an order of magnitude less than the compressive values, but these strengths are in turn an order of magnitude greater than the tensile strength of the mortar used as grout between the imperfectly finished surfaces of the medieval ashlar.[2] It is, therefore, important to give attention to the general properties of medieval mortars.

The literature on the history of architecture is often misleading about medieval mortars; many discussions of the processes and consequences of how mortar "dries" contradict one another. For instance, medieval mortars, which are assumed here to be basically pure lime (or lime and sand mixtures) having no hydraulic properties, have been described as taking anywhere from months to centuries to dry.[3] In fact, lime mortar passes through two separate stages, setting and carbonation. Carbonation can be a very slow process and bears no relation to drying. Only setting, which is short-term by comparison, matches the ordinary sense of "drying."

Lime mortar is produced by adding water to quicklime, a lime powder made from burnt limestone. The water combines with the lime (calcium oxide) to form hydrated lime (calcium hydroxide). Excess water then produces a mortar paste composed of microcrystals of calcium hydroxide. This pure lime mortar paste is said to be set when all the water has been evaporated into the atmosphere or absorbed into surrounding masonry blocks.[4] The length of time taken by this process varies with the amount of excess water, the relative humidity, and the absorption rates of the stone. Though lime mortar is described as "slow-setting," this is only in contrast to Portland cement, which will set within about ten hours.[5] Mortar may take days or perhaps weeks to dry, but certainly not years.

Carbonation, the second process affecting lime mortars, is by contrast very slow. The set mortar paste, calcium hydroxide, reacts with carbon dioxide to form calcium carbonate, the basic constituent of limestone. The process is slow under ordinary circumstances because the percentage of carbon dioxide in the atmosphere is low. In addition, diffusion of carbon dioxide beyond a thin surface of carbonated mortar deep into masonry occurs at a very slow rate, if at all. Quite possibly much of the mortar within medieval masonry is uncarbonated to this day. Such masonry has to rely on the strength of the set mortar, not on that of the carbonated lime (limestone) mortar, for practically all the mortar is uncarbonated for a long time and perhaps at no time is it entirely carbonated.[6]

Lime mortar that is only set is not very strong, even in compression. However, neither the strength of the mortar nor of the masonry blocks is as important as the properties of their combined construction. The strengths and deformation characteristics of medieval construction are difficult to predict, since those of the constituent elements are not well known. Indeed test results on discrete samples of materials are not accurate indicators of the behavior of the same materials when they are used in large quantities in buildings. Studies of masonry walls loaded perpendicular to the mortar bed have shown that mortar can survive in conditions where its simple crushing strength is exceeded by as much as 300 percent.[7] In my own observations of medieval construction, I have never discerned any crushing failure of the masonry, only distress caused by tension. It is the tensile forces leading to this mode of distress, therefore, that most need investigating.

DESIGN OF EXPERIMENTS

In modeling a building to determine how forces are distributed within its structure, its actual structural configuration is first abstracted to its most basic form in order to simplify the analysis as much as possible. Analysis of the long, straight portions of Gothic churches is facilitated by their repeating modular, bay design (figure 11). The buildings can be considered to be supported by a series of parallel, transverse "frames" consisting of the principal load-bearing structural elements: piers, buttresses, lateral walls, and ribbed vaults. These "frames" are reproduced in the model because they are usually representative of the most critical structural solution of a particular church. The ends of the straight portions of the churches, on the other hand, are atypical because they are generally supported by structures arrayed in more than a single plane, which gives them additional stiffness and strength. They are, therefore, rarely subject to the problems found in the more open,

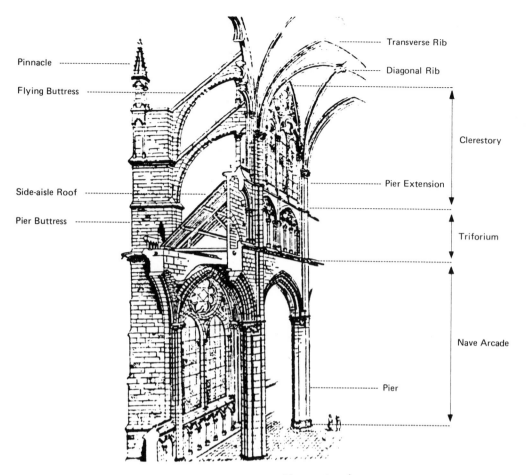

Pinnacle

Flying Buttress

Side-aisle Roof

Pier Buttress

Transverse Rib

Diagonal Rib

Clerestory

Pier Extension

Triforium

Nave Arcade

Pier

11 Nave section of
Amiens Cathedral, as
drawn by Viollet-le-Duc,
illustrating Gothic
construction and
nomenclature.

straight bay sections. Indeed, when the vaults of the straight bays of Beauvais collapsed in 1284 (see chapter 5), the structure of the rounded eastern end of the building remained firm, and it stands today essentially as it was originally constructed.

Research at Princeton during the 1960s demonstrated that tests of small-scale plastic models could be used to predict internal forces within reinforced concrete structures subjected to normal, in-service loadings, even though concrete is notoriously inelastic, compositionally inhomogeneous, and subject to tensile microcracking.[8] Experience with the concrete structures led to the idea that masonry buildings might also be amenable to investigation using small-scale models, but only if the masonry, like the model, acted essentially as a monolith. This is true if all the individual stones within the masonry are pressed against adjacent stones by compressive forces set up in the interior of the structure in response to environmental loadings. In fact, this assumption coincides with criteria for successful medieval masonry performance because the tensile strength of medieval mortar is so low that structural continuity cannot be maintained in the masonry if any substantial amount of tensile stress is present. The presumption that all of the masonry within the structure of a Gothic church acts in compression, however, must still be confirmed by the model test results.

This approach to modeling is analogous to the strategy of the mathematician who assumes the *form* of a solution to an equation and then tests the validity of the solution to confirm the initial assumption. In the same way that the mathematician may find it necessary to alter the form of the initial assumption, the model of a building's section can be altered by slitting it in the indicated regions of tension so that the effect of tensile cracking in the masonry is represented. This additional step, however, has been found generally to be unnecessary; although an important aim of the studies is to locate possible regions of tension, if they do exist, they are usually highly localized. Compression does in fact prevail in all of the medieval buildings that we have analyzed.

Although modeling methods are most often used to find localized stress concentrations, for example, in airframe analysis, in the case of medieval buildings general force distributions throughout the structure are sought. No effort is therefore generally made to represent the actual cross sections of component structural elements in detail.[9] Even the action of the cross-ribbed vault, a three-dimensional structure, is simulated in the models as a planar arch.[10] The surcharge, normally composed of rubble and mortar placed above the haunches of a vault (shown as "rubble fill" in figure 66), is considered to act as solid fill, transferring vault thrusts to the pier extensions and to the buttressing system and, conversely, helping to support the pier extensions against inward-acting forces such as high winds on the windward clerestory and roof. The heavily loaded, massive footings are also assumed to give complete fixity to the bases of the piers. (The extensive footing beneath a Gothic cathedral pier is described in note 5 of chapter 4.)

Another assumption made in this type of analysis is that gravity begins to act only after construction is completed. This is, in fact, the case with respect to vaulting and flying buttresses. These structures were usually assembled on rigid centering and hence were not subject to dead-weight loadings until they were complete and the centering was removed. At the other end of the time scale, dead-weight loadings can cause unrecoverable viscous flow (creep) of the masonry over a long period whereas wind loadings, which are of variable magnitude and come from every quarter, do not. In any event, if the basic support and form of a structure remain unchanged with time, the distribution of internal forces will alter little.[11] The initial elastic distribution indicated by the model can therefore safely be taken to remain the same even over the long term.

LOADINGS

All of the model studies described here investigate the effects of the dead-weight loading of the building and the action of high winds impinging on the building fabric. They do not consider the forces within the building structure that can be caused by dislocations arising from differential thermal expansion as the sun heats portions of the structure, partial settlement, or the sequence of construction. The latter effect, in particular, would be extremely difficult to examine in the absence of records dating from the time of building. And, in any case, these loadings are not of central interest in historical studies that are concerned primarily with the raison d'être of structural forms created by medieval designers in response to loadings of which they could not fail to have been aware.

The distribution of dead weight within a structure is usually calculated by, first, determining from overall and detailed building drawings, when available, the volume of stone and the placement of the centers of gravity of the individual building elements—the loadings are then found by multiplying these volumes by a normal density of stone, 2,400 kg/m³ (150 lbs/in³); second, determining surface areas of flat materials such as glass in large wall openings or lead sheathing on roofs, estimating their thickness, and multiplying the resulting volumes by appropriate densities taken from standard values of unit weights; and third, estimating, from detailed drawings, quantities and sizes of timber roof framing to determine the weight of roof trusses. Occasionally, one is fortunate enough to find all of this information in the literature on a particular building (as was the case, for example, for a bay in the nave of Palma Cathedral, as described in chapter 7); then it is only necessary to perform a few checks to confirm its validity. Only those loadings that can cause significant bending within the building "frame" need be represented on the model; the effect of loadings,

such as the weight of concentric piers, can be easily accounted for analytically and added later to the results from the tests of the model.

The data needed to estimate wind-load distributions on a tall building include, first, local meteorological records giving general wind speed and direction; second, theoretical wind velocity profiles (velocity variation according to height above ground level) for the particular terrain of the building site; and third, wind pressure distribution calculations based on data from the first two categories as well as on the configuration of the building. Wind velocity data over long periods of time, even as long as a century, can usually be obtained from governmental meteorological sources.[12] Maximum wind speeds normally occur over a fairly wide azimuth so that the full wind loadings are considered to act transversely to the building's longitudinal axis. The profile of wind velocity shown in figure 12 over level terrain is for "surface roughness" assumed to correspond to a medieval city at the time of Gothic church construction.[13]

With these data assembled, wind pressures (and suction forces on the leeward side) of the building are then found from an equation having the form:

$$p = \tfrac{1}{2}\rho \cdot V^2 \cdot C \cdot G \qquad (1)$$

where

p = wind pressure
ρ = mass density of air, taken as 0.135 kg-sec²/m⁴ (0.00256 lb-sec²/ft⁴)
V = wind velocity
C = variable, nondimensional coefficient related to building form
G = gust factor to account for dynamic action of impinging air

The distribution of the pressure coefficient C across the surface of buildings is established by assuming the approximate configuration shown in figure 13. To obtain the coefficients, the results of two separate series of wind tunnel tests were

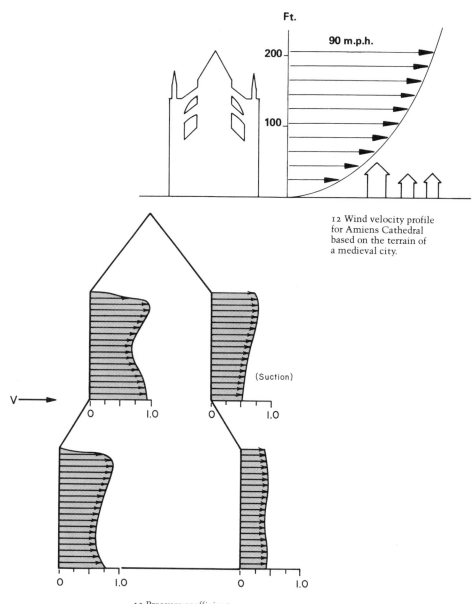

Ft.

90 m.p.h.

200

100

12 Wind velocity profile
for Amiens Cathedral
based on the terrain of
a medieval city.

V →

(Suction)

0   1.0   0   1.0

0   1.0   0   1.0

13 Pressure coefficient
distribution for typical
Gothic church configura-
tion based on wind tun-
nel test data. The effect
of discontinuities in
the outer fabric (e.g., the
buttressing system) is
omitted.

used. The first, carried out at the University of Iowa, gave data on primary building forms placed within a constant velocity field.[14] The second, performed at the University of Toronto, studied the effect of the variation in wind velocity that occurs when changes in building height produce flow reversals and eddy formations not present in a constant velocity field.[15] The Iowa data, modified by information from the Toronto tests, yielded the pressure coefficient distribution for Amiens, as illustrated in figure 13. This distribution was based on a roof wind velocity of 145 km/hr (90 mph) rather than on velocities at particular elevations. No wind-tunnel data were available for highly pitched roofs (nave roofs sloped at about 60 degrees), so pressure distributions were estimated on the basis of assumed airflow patterns. Distributions for the side aisle roofs also had to be assumed.

The gust factor (G), which takes into account height-to-width aspect ratio, the natural frequency and damping of the structure, the roughness of background terrain, and gust energy based on wind wave distributions, offers a relatively simple way to measure the dynamic influence of the wind. This action includes buffeting by gusts; buffeting by turbulence and vortices shed by the structure itself; buffeting by the wake from another structure; and aerodynamic damping. When the total height of the structure is less than one-seventh of the gust wave length—generally 300–900 m (1,000–3,000 ft)—a constant gust factor can be applied for the entire structure. A gust factor of 2.3 was calculated for Amiens, one of the largest Gothic churches, and the factor 2.2 was derived for the smallest church analyzed—St. Ouen, Rouen. Hence all of the buildings treated here may be considered to fall within this small range, and gust factors of this magnitude probably account for the maximum possible dynamic effect of wind on this type of building.

The wind pressure distribution found to be acting on a typical bay in the nave of Amiens is shown in figure 14. The maximum total lateral loadings from pressure (and suction) acting against this bay were estimated to be 150,000 kg (330,000 lbs). For comparison, the total deadweight loads of each bay were computed to be 2.8×10^6 kg (6.1 million lbs). For modeling purposes, the timber roof structure is assumed to be rigid enough so that its full wind loading is equally applied to both sides at the point of its attachment to the upper portion (parapet wall) of the clerestory. The roof, however, is not considered to provide a rigid connective brace between the clerestory walls. This connection in the model is made solely by the simulated high vault. Dynamic loadings caused by oscillations or vibrations of the roof structure are considered negligible because of its extremely heavy construction.

SCALING THEORY

Dimensional analysis, developed as an offshoot of theoretical physics, provides a powerful tool for both designing experiments with small-scale models and for scaling the behavior of the model to the full-scale prototype. For the static or quasi-static loadings to which large masonry buildings are subjected over their normal life spans, scaling theory based on dimensional analysis indicates that if all model dimensions are kept in *scale* with those of the prototype, if the *distribution* of loadings to the model is the same as the prototype load distribution, and if the *behavior* of the model's materials is the same as that of the material of the prototype,[16] there exists a set of dimensionless (unitless) parametric terms relating the dimensions of the structure and the loadings acting on it to the resulting internal forces which apply to both the model and prototype. For instance, a dimensionless parameter relating force per unit length (f) along the edge of a pier buttress[17] to the total loading on the building (F) and its overall height (L) is $f \cdot L/F$. Since this

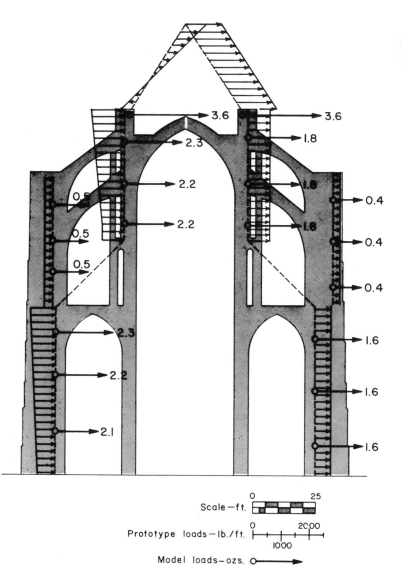

14 Full-scale and model wind loads for Amiens bay configuration derived from equation (1).

Scale—ft. 0 ____ 25

Prototype loads—lb./ft. 0 ____ 1000 ____ 2000

Model loads—ozs. ○——→

parametric term applies to both the full-scale prototype (represented by the subscript p) and the scaled model (represented by subscript m):

$$f_p \cdot L_p/F_p = f_m \cdot L_m/F_m \qquad (2)$$

and this identity yields:

$$f_p = f_m \cdot (F_m/F_p)^{-1} \cdot (L_m/L_p) \qquad (3)$$

where

(F_m/F_p) = loading scale factor (model to prototype)
(L_m/L_p) = dimensional scale factor (model to prototype)

Note that equation (3), relating the prototype to behavior observed in the model, applies to any ratio of model-to-prototype loading. The model's loading is merely limited to a range that will preserve it from appreciable distortion. Hence the magnitude of the loads may be selected to yield convenient experimental data. An example of the application of the scaling law to analyze a structural element of Amiens Cathedral is given at the end of the following section.

PHOTOELASTIC MODELING

The development of reliable, accurate experimental stress analysis techniques was given impetus during the Second World War by the demand for increasingly sophisticated aircraft components and in the decades after the war by the requirements of the nuclear power industry. Probably the most important single advance came with the introduction of electric strain gauges, which can very accurately measure response in both a full-scale structure and a model. Yet because gauges provide information only at the points where they are applied, they are not as advantageous for structural modeling as the somewhat less precise but far more informative full-field optical methods. These techniques give a clear view of *overall* structural behavior and facilitate recognition of previously unsuspected critical regions within the structure. Moreover they permit the investigation of highly localized stress concentrations even with small models. These advantages have led to the refinement and simplification of the most venerable, but probably the most powerful, of the optical modeling techniques, photoelasticity, based on observation in polarized light of transparent models.[18]

By the mid-1960s the advantages and the general reliability of photoelastic modeling for the analysis of mechanical components was well understood and accepted. The 1964 edition of the *Boiler and Pressure Vessel Code*, published by the American Society of Mechanical Engineers, specified that the technique was to be used for the structural analysis of nuclear reactor containment vessels.[19] Yet photoelasticity had rarely been used in this country to study building structures until we began, as part of our research using small-scale models, to apply it to determine the structural behavior of thin-shell concrete roofs,[20] and following the success of this experience, to apply the technique in the analysis of a series of Gothic buildings.

Photoelastic modeling is applicable for planar (two-dimensional) or three-dimensional structural studies. The model loading method described is that generally used for three-dimensional models; however its advantages led also to its use for the two-dimensional models discussed in this text.

All the models are fabricated from stress-free epoxy plastic. Cast sheets are used for the two-dimensional models, which are then formed using a contour router.[21] More complex three-dimensional elements, such as the vault models formed from cylindrical castings as described in chapter 8, are shaped with conventional, metal-working machine tools. The overall size of the planar model sections is about 25 cm (10 in) square for the smaller buildings and about 40 cm (16 in) square for the larger ones. The size of the base enclosed by the three-dimensional model used for the vault study is 28 cm (11 in) square.

Following their fabrication, the models are loaded with weights scaled to represent the loadings acting on the full-scale building. Figure 15 illustrates the technique for dead-weight loading of a two-dimensional model. In the figure, the model of Beauvais Cathedral is partially loaded to represent the effect of vault, buttress, and upper pier loadings (the effect of the weight of the lower portions of the piers was accounted for analytically). To simplify the experiment, the total load applied to the Beauvais model, 4.40 kg (9.70 lbs), was inverted, that is, the model was placed in tension rather than in the compression to which the actual structure is subjected. The *distribution* of forces within the model is exactly the same whether it is in tension or compression, and the additional bracing needed to prevent possible out-of-plane buckling of the thin model under compression can be dispensed with. The analyst need only bear in mind that, with the inverted loading, compression in the model corresponds to tension in the actual building.

The actual, distributed deadweight and wind loadings are considered to act at discrete points. Figure 14 illustrates how the wind loading acting on a bay of Amiens Cathedral is reduced in scale and simulated by an array of discrete loadings — with the total loading chosen to produce good optical activity without unduly distorting the model. The model loads shown in this figure, representing 1:135,000 of the full-scale wind loading, are simulated on the model in figure 16.

The loaded models are placed in an oven as the first step in a process known as "stress-freezing." They are gradually heated to about 150° Celsius. At this temperature, the epoxy changes from its room temperature "glassy" condition to a "rubbery" state and the loadings cause it to deform. These deformations are locked in when the model is slowly cooled, and the epoxy returns to its glassy state. When the model is cool, the loadings are removed and the effect of the locked-in strains can be detected as patterns of light and dark

(or of color when a white-light source is used) with the use of a polarizing-light instrument called a polariscope. These patterns can be read as contour maps of strain that, since strain is directly related to force intensity, can be interpreted as showing the force distributions within the model. The maps, or interference patterns, can then be photographed to provide a comprehensive record of the model's behavior.[22] Once examined and photographed, the models can be used again with different loadings because any prior pattern is erased when they are reheated with a new loading array. Three-dimensional models cannot be readily reused, however, because, in order to examine patterns internal to the structure, slices must be cut from the model for observation in the polariscope.

The principles of the polariscope used to observe the interference patterns in the model are illustrated in figure 17 and a polariscope, which I designed with a dual light source (for white or monochromatic green light), is illustrated in figure 18.[23] Under white light illumination each area in the interference pattern is characterized by a distinctive color indicating a specific order of interference (see, for example, plate 2) and representing a different magnitude of force intensity: the color of the dark background field is order zero, blue is order one, magenta is two, and so on. In monochromatic light, the interference pattern appears as successive dark and light lines (see figure 31).

Both the monochromatic and color photoelastic interference patterns may be interpreted both qualitatively and quantitatively. Examples of qualitative determination are: generally regions of highest local stress are indicated by close spacing of the lines (for example, at the base of the Amiens piers where $N = 6.0$ in figure 31); bending patterns are typically characterized by almost parallel lines along the axis of the members[24] (for example, in the piers and flying buttresses of figure 31); and, conversely, freedom from bending

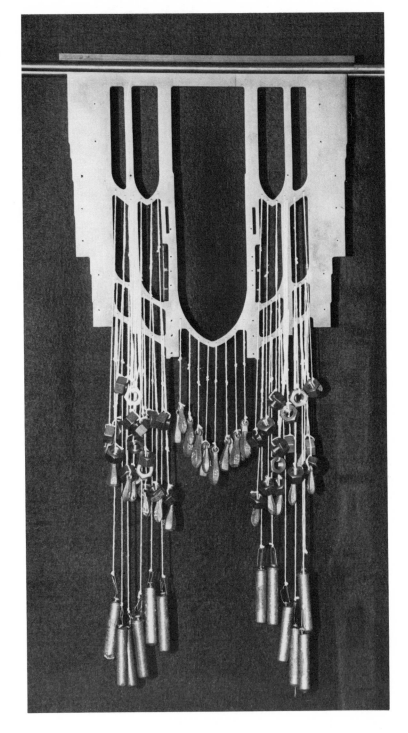

15 Beauvais Cathedral
model under simulated
partial dead-weight load-
ing. Photo by K. Bakhtar.

16 Amiens Cathedral
model under simulated
wind loading. Vertically
hung weights attached to
45-degree spring lines
produce the horizontal
model loadings. Photo by
M. Goro, *Life*.

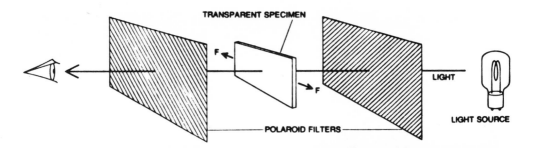

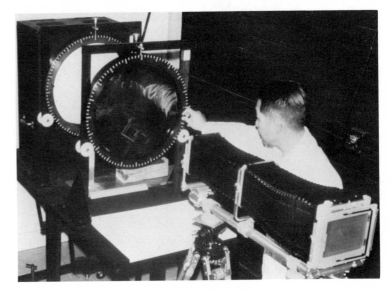

17 Principle of photo-
elastic observation. The
stretched, transparent
specimen (acted upon by
forces, *F*), placed between
crossed polarizing filters,
displays to the viewer
an interference pattern
related to stress distri-
bution.

18 A 45-cm-diameter
field, dual light-source
polariscope designed
by the author. Photo
courtesy of the Naval
Civil Engineering
Laboratory.

is indicated by the absence of lines (for example, almost pure axial loading (compression) is indicated in the piers of Palma Cathedral in plate 10).

For quantitative analysis, photographs of the interference patterns permit the analyst to identify and give fractional numerical values to points that lie between the interference contours (this is best accomplished with the monochromatic patterns), thereby refining the model data. The intensity of force at any point on the model (f) is then derived by multiplying the order of interference (N) by a calibration factor (K) obtained from a specimen of the model material subjected to a known force distribution under the same test conditions as the model.[25]

An illustration of the application of these formulations is given by the analysis for stress in the Amiens pier buttress under wind loading (figure 31). Since the force along the edge of the model (f_m) is given by multiplying the interference order (N) by the calibration factor (K), equation (3) may be rewritten as

$$f_p = N \cdot K \cdot (F_m/F_p)^{-1} \cdot (L_m/L_p) \qquad (4)$$

The stress at a point in the buttress is then derived from dividing the force per unit length (f_p) by the width of the buttress at that point. At the point in the pier where the corresponding model interference order (N) is 2.0—and from calibration it is known that the model material has a sensitivity (K) of 0.360 kg/order-cm (2.01 lbs/order-in)—the model loading scale factor is 1:135,000, and the dimensional scale factor is 1:136, equation (4) yields $f_p = 715$ kg/cm (3990 lbs/in). The stress in the pier buttress, which is 180 cm (70 in) wide at this point, is therefore 715 kg/cm divided by 180 cm, yielding 4.0 kg/cm² (57 psi). Figure 32, which shows the forces along the entire edge of the pier buttress of Amiens Cathedral, was derived in this manner.

The techniques described are those that would be employed in the engineering analysis of complex modern structures. Such analyses are based on detailed knowledge of the building's configuration, the behavior of its construction materials, and the environmental conditions to which it is subject. Although quantitative methods of this type are not usually applied to the study of historic architecture, the accounts that follow demonstrate the power of the methodology particularly for buildings having the structural complexity of a High Gothic cathedral.

NOTES

An introductory explanation of the basic behavior of structures and their analysis is given in the glossary. Recommended simple texts on this subject, in order of increasing analytical complexity, are Mario Salvadori and Robert Heller, *Structure in Architecture* (Englewood Cliffs, N.J.: Prentice-Hall, 1963); William Morgan, *The Elements of Structure* (London: Pitman, 1964); and Daniel L. Schodek, *Structures* (Englewood Cliffs, N.J.: Prentice-Hall, 1980).

For further information on photoelastic modeling and other optical stress analysis techniques, see James W. Dally and William F. Riley, *Experimental Stress Analysis,* 2nd ed. (New York: McGraw-Hill, 1978); on dimensional analysis, see P. W. Bridgeman, *Dimensional Analysis (New Haven: Yale University Press,* 1931); and on wind loading, see Emil Semiu and Robert H. Scanlan, *Wind Effects on Structures* (New York: Wiley-Interscience, 1978).

1 Studies of the cathedrals of Chartres and Metz based on the general approach developed in this chapter but using finite-element computer modeling, as described in chapter 8, were carried out by Lutz Kübler ("Computeranalyse der Statik zweier gotischen Kathedralen," *Architectura* 4.2 [1974]:97–111), who reported good agreement with our earlier photoelastic model study of Chartres.

2 See Ronald C. Smith, *Materials of Construction* (New York: McGraw-Hill, 1973), p. 165. Henri Masson ("Le Rationalisme dans l'Architecture du Moyen Age," *Bulletin Monumental* LXXVI [1912]), reports tests of medieval mortar giving tensile strengths of 2 kg/cm² (30 psi).

3 John Fitchen ("Appendix G: The Slow Setting Time of Medieval Mortars and its Consequences," *The Construction of Gothic Cathedrals* [Oxford: Clarendon Press, 1961], pp. 262–265) cites the lowest figure, "a minimum of six months," from H. and E. Ranquet, "Origine française du berceau roman," *Bulletin Monumental* XC (1931):45. The highest is contained in the claim that "in walls of great thickness, centuries can pass before the final set is acquired" (Pol Abraham, "Les données plastiques et fonctionnelles du problème de l'ogive," *Recherche No. 1: Le Problème de l'ogive* [Paris, 1939]:36.

A mortar has hydraulic properties if it will set under water. Roman pozzolana cements and modern Portland cement are hydraulic. Medieval mortars that were made by burning limestone containing clay, blue lias limestone, chalk marls, or grey chalk could have had hydraulic or semihydraulic properties (see Ministry of Public Building and Works, *Lime for Building,* 3rd ed. [London: HMSO, 1970]). The likely medieval building practice of keeping hydrated lime in tubs with a water layer at the top during a period of construction, however, guaranteed that the mortar would lose even semihydraulic properties during storage.

4 Freshly quarried stone is "green" with ground water—"quarry sap," which evaporates during its exposure to the atmosphere. See Robert J. Schaffer, *The Weathering of Natural Building Stones* (Watford: Garston, 1972), p. 15. Rates of absorption for bricks and building stones vary according to their natural properties and moisture content; but all absorb considerable amounts of water and set a mortar under normal circumstances. See Sven Sahlin, *Structural Masonry* (Englewood Cliffs, N.J.: Prentice-Hall, 1971), pp. 12ff.

5 Sahlin, *Structural Masonry,* p. 19.

6 For a detailed discussion of the chemistry, see Frederick M. Lea, *The Chemistry of Cement and Concrete,* 3rd ed. (London: E. Arnold & Company, 1970), pp. 29ff.

7 Sahlin, *Structural Masonry,* pp. 52–56.

8 Robert Mark, "Photomechanical Model Analysis of Concrete Structures," in *Models for Concrete Structures* (Detroit: American Concrete Institute, 1970), pp. 187–214.

9 Solid dressed stone was used for the construction of many critical structural elements such as the flying buttresses and the piers of High Gothic churches. Some structural elements, however, were formed of a rubble and mortar core encased in dressed stone. For purposes of modeling, this distinction has not been taken into account as doing so would not greatly affect the resulting force distributions.

10 The true action of the ribbed vault is partially accounted for by deepening the modeled rib in order to have the same scaled stiffness as the total of all the transverse and diagonal ribs meeting the pier extension, each rib being attached to a strip of web four times its width.

11 This phenomenon also underlies the use of models made of certain viscoelastic plastics in order to predict elastic response. See Raymond D. Midlin, "A Mathematical Theory of Photoviscoelasticity," *Journal of Applied Physics* 20 (1949):206–216.

12 In this country, velocity data are now usually given by the quantity "fastest mile," the maximum velocity of a mile-long column of air passing a reference point. This is done to represent better the mean wind conditions and to make this information easier to combine with the gust factor in equation (1).

13 Alan G. Davenport, "The Relationship of Wind Structure to Wind Loading," in *Wind Effects on Buildings and Structures* (London: HMSO, 1963), pp. 53–103.

14 N. Chien, Y. Feng, H. H. Want, and T. T. Siao, "Wind Tunnel Studies of Pressure Distribution on Elementary Building Forms," Institute of Hydraulics Research, University of Iowa, Ames, Iowa, 1951.

15 Alan G. Davenport, "The Treatment of Wind Loads on Tall Buildings," *Tall Buildings*, edited by A. Coull and B. Stafford Smith (New York: Pergamon Press, 1967).

16 As with finding force distributions (rather than local stress distributions) from plastic models of reinforced concrete structures, these criteria may be interpreted as *gross* behavior. The best check on model-prototype compatibility is derived from comparing model predictions with measured prototype performance. This has been done with reinforced concrete structures (see note 8). No similar measurements are available for medieval masonry construction, but subsequent confirmations by on-site observation of model predictions of local tension provides a measure of confidence.

17 The force intensity (f), called a "stress resultant" in texts on shell theory, is defined as the integral of the stress over the thickness. Since the stress in a planar model is constant through the model thickness, it is most convenient when using optical models to measure this quantity directly and then to determine the model stress, if needed, merely by dividing f by the model thickness.

18 The photoelastic effect was first reported in the early nineteenth century by Sir David Brewster in *Philosophical Transactions* (1815), p. 60. James Clerk Maxwell read a paper in 1850 before the Royal Society of Edinburgh in which he described a photoelastic experiment using "jelly of isinglass" as a model material. Photoelasticity, however, did not become a practical engineering tool until the 1930s with the development of plastics that were optically sensitive and easily formed into models.

19 American Society of Mechanical Engineers, *ASME Boiler and Pressure Vessel Code*, Section III, "Nuclear Vessels" (New York: 1965), p. 107.

20 David P. Billington and Robert Mark, "Small Scale Model Analysis of Thin Shells," *Journal of the American Concrete Institute* 62 (June 1965):673–688.

21 In this process, an aluminum template of about 0.3 cm (one-eighth in) thickness is first fabricated. The template is then attached to the roughly-cut-to-form plastic sheet with double-sided contact tape in preparation for routing.

22 Monochromatic interference patterns were photographed using 102 × 127 mm (4 × 5) back camera with a long-focal-length process lens and an interference filter. Typical exposure time is 40 seconds at f/32 with Polaroid 3000 ASA film. For color photography, typical data are one-second exposure at f/8 with 25 ASA color film using the unfiltered white light source and a 35 mm camera.

23 Further instrument details may be found in Robert Mark, "Dual Light Source for a Large Field Diffused Light Polariscope," *Review of the Scientific Instruments* 35 (April 1964): 521–522.

24 The identification of tension or compression resulting from bending can usually be detected simply from the curvature of the model's edge (convex signifies bending tension; concave indicates compression). A more general method for determining tension or compression is based on observing the shift of the model interference patterns while rotating one of the polarizing filters of the polariscope (August J. Durelli and William F. Riley, *Introduction to Photomechanics* (Englewood Cliffs, N.J.: Prentice-Hall, 1965), pp. 92–94). This determination must be made directly with the model in the polariscope; the interference pattern photographs themselves do not contain sufficient information to indicate if the model forces are compressive or tensile.

25 This relationship applies only along the boundary of a member. But since the boundary forces in structures are critical in practically all instances, this limitation need not concern us. The dimensional units of the boundary force (f) are force/unit-length. Hence the units of the calibration factor (K) are force/order-unit-length. Calibration techniques are described in Dally and Riley, *Experimental Stress Analysis*.

3

THE BEGINNING OF HIGH GOTHIC: THE CATHEDRALS OF CHARTRES AND BOURGES

Construction of the cathedrals at Chartres and Bourges began almost simultaneously: 1194 for Chartres and 1195 for Bourges. At Bourges construction proceeded in the usual manner, from east to west. The choir was completed in 1214, although other construction was not completed for almost a century. The much more rapid pace of construction at Chartres brought work on the entire main vessel of the cathedral to a close in 1221.[1] Dimensions of the buildings are very similar; the height of the vaults of both is about 46 m (118 ft). But Chartres has three aisles and a transept between the nave and choir, whereas Bourges has five continuous aisles and no transept.

Chartres is a very impressive building, particularly in its details, and it has always been greatly admired. After some initial resistance, its form was accepted as the standard for Gothic church design, ending the period of wide experimentation with church building forms that character-ized the twelfth century.[2] On the other hand, although Bourges has always been esteemed for its imposing size and beauty (plate 1), it has never attracted such an extensive following. The importance of Chartres is implicit in the emphasis placed on it in the literature on the Gothic cathe-dral. Bourges, often mentioned as an inter-esting footnote, has been the subject of only one complete modern study, by the architectural historian Robert Branner.[3] The main reason for the ascendancy of Chartres, according to Branner, was that it was imitable: its design could be replicated at any scale to suit almost any site; the Bourges spatial scheme could only be adopted whole and at a very large scale.

When Chartres and Bourges were in con-struction, exposed flying buttresses were a relatively new device. Although they were probably first employed before 1180 at Notre Dame in Paris, their full potential for allowing a great reduction of clere-story wall was only realized at Chartres and Bourges. Cross sections of the two buildings, however, reveal that their designers employed very different forms of buttressing (figure 19).[4] At Chartres

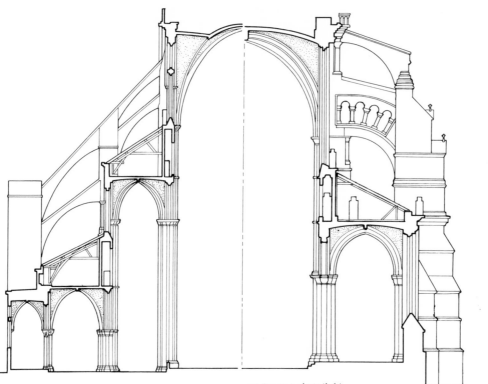

19 Bourges choir (left)
and Chartres nave (right).
Comparative cross
sections.

20 Chartres nave buttressing. Flying buttresses are almost hidden by the massive pier buttresses. Photo by J. Hart.

the entire system is massive except for the relatively light upper flyers (figure 20). Each of the tall pier buttresses, exclusive of its foundation, weighs about 1 million kg (2.2 million lbs). At Bourges, on the other hand, a series of fine, steeply sloped flyers is supported by low pier buttresses, each weighing but 400,000 kg (880,000 lbs) (figure 21).

The present chapter is concerned with what lay behind these different approaches to structure in two giant cathedrals built in the same region and at the same time.

THE NAVE OF CHARTRES

As with every other feature of Chartres, much has been written of its structure, particularly its use of flying buttresses. According to Paul Frankl, "the master who rebuilt the cathedral at Chartres . . . was the first man to draw the logical consequences from the construction of flying buttresses."[5] In the same vein, George Henderson writes in a more recent text on Chartres: "The architect . . . recognized in the flying buttress a great new device whereby he might radically reorganize the whole appearance of a church interior, and at one stroke achieve simplicity, unity, coherence. From the moment when he took command of work at Chartres he had flying buttresses and their logical employment in mind."[6] The view of still another influential writer, Otto von Simson, is that "the flying buttresses of Chartres are the first to have been conceived, not only structurally but also aesthetically, as integral parts of the overall design."[7] Almost all the writers, however, question the role of the light upper flyers at roof level (figure 22). Some maintain that the upper flyers are purely decorative. Others believe that they function as structure, although there is disagreement about how they do so.

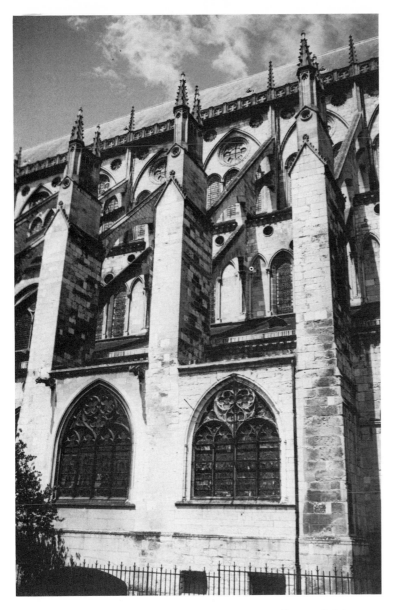

21 Bourges choir buttressing. The lightness
of the buttressing system
in a building of this size
is unique.

22 Chartres nave. The
upper flying buttresses
were thought to have
been added in the four-
teenth century.

Viollet-le-Duc appears to have been the first to take the view that the upper flying buttresses at Chartres were not part of the original building and were therefore introduced to solve a problem in the structure that appeared later. In his article on the flying buttress, he discussed only the lower flyers and included a drawing that omitted the upper flyers altogether (figure 23).[8] His argument was based on a document written in 1316 by a group of experts who had gathered to examine the fabric of the century-old cathedral. Viollet-le-Duc and many after him have generally interpreted this document as a recommendation for the construction of additional flying buttresses.

Viollet-le-Duc's interpretation has, however, been challenged by others, including my co-worker, Alan Borg, who carefully reexamined the 1316 document and assembled archaeological evidence to indicate that the upper flyers at Chartres had been part of the original construction.[9] Even if this was the case, the functional reason for their existence still requires explanation. We know that they were not necessary to counteract the dead-load weight of the roof because medieval roof framing is tied between the parapets that support it by stout, pinned timbers. There is, therefore, no outward-acting horizontal thrust from the roof weight as there is from the vaulting. In the absence of this thrust, however, wind action will create lateral loads that are transmitted to the upper portion of the pier extensions. Thus Viollet-le-Duc's argument that the upper flyers were added after 1316 to correct a fault in the original configuration might be substantiated if it could be shown that they significantly reduced local tensile forces in the pier extension caused by wind loadings on the high roof. Tests of the model of the nave were therefore directed to an examination of the response of the pier extensions to wind action—with and without the upper flyers in place.

23 Chartres nave. Buttressing without the upper flyers (after Viollet-le-Duc).

To examine the pier extension response, one-hundred-year meteorological data for the Paris region were obtained (Chartres is 80 km from Paris). A scale model of a typical nave "frame" section of Chartres (as shown in figure 19) was fabricated without the upper flyers and tested under a loading that represented the actual distribution of wind pressure (and suction on the lee side).[10] The internal force distributions were determined from photo-elastic observation as described in chapter 2. Following this first test, the model was annealed by heating to restore it to its undeformed condition and the scaled upper flyers were attached with high-temperature epoxy cement. A second test was then made with the same simulated wind loading to produce the interference pattern shown in plate 2.

In the final phase of the analysis, a calculation was made of the stress in the pier extensions caused by the dead-weight loading of the roof and its framing, the weight of that portion of the structure of the bay supported by the pier extensions above the critical sections, and the weight of the heavy longitudinal arches above the clerestory windows. Combining this dead-weight effect with the stresses arising from extreme wind forces gave the maximum stresses that could be anticipated in the structure.

All of the compression values in the buttress region were much lower than typical stresses at the pier bases. Hence they were not critical, and they required no further consideration. Low tensile stresses, however, were indicated at the windward edges of the windward pier extensions just above the middle tier of the flying buttresses at the base of the colonnettes that provide support to the upper flyers. The onset of this tension in the section without flying buttresses was found to correspond to gusts with a mean velocity at rooftop level of 70 km/hr (44 mph). When the upper wall of the clerestory was supported by the flying buttresses, however, no tension appeared until the

wind reached 90 km/hr (56 mph). The buttresses were, therefore, effective in improving the resistance of the pier extensions to high winds.

But they were not totally effective. Under the most extreme gust conditions, with mean velocities of 105 km/hr (65 mph) near ground level and 135 km/hr (84 mph) at rooftop level, maximum tensile stress, which reached 4 kg/cm² (57 psi) in the pier extension of the section without the buttresses, still reached 2 kg/cm² (28 psi) in the buttressed section. Although these are relatively low magnitudes, cracking distress in mortar can occur with a tensile stress of only 2 kg/cm². One would expect, therefore, to find evidence of distress in the cathedral's fabric, even with the upper flying buttresses in place, although the relatively low values of the indicated stress and the nature of the bending stress distribution across the section of the pier extension would mean that the distress would most likely be confined to the outermost courses of stone.

This finding was borne out by observation of the cathedral itself. During a site visit in 1971, soon after the analysis was performed, I discovered that stone in the critical region at the base of the colonnettes had recently been replaced. The supervising architect for the cathedral at that time, M. Louis Esnault, confirmed that this was part of a systematic program of repair in that area of the fabric.[11]

It is possible to conclude, then, that in the absence of the upper flying buttresses, the pier extensions would have shown tension under the effect of relatively lower wind velocities and the probability of distress in the piers would certainly have been greater. But, as it has been necessary to replace the stones, the upper flyers do not entirely eliminate the problem of tension. Evidently they are too light a structure to have been a deliberate addition intended to rectify an obvious structural flaw.

Under these circumstances, it becomes difficult to believe that the experts of 1316 would have suggested the addition of this type of buttress. By that date, architects had considerable practical experience with buttressing and they would hardly have proposed the difficult and expensive addition of extra flyers unless they were convinced that they would be effective. It therefore seems more likely that Viollet-le-Duc was in error and that the upper flyers were, in fact, part of the original construction, a conclusion borne out by the archaeological evidence.

The significance of the analysis, however, goes beyond the apparently minor issue of the date and purpose of the upper flyers at Chartres. The findings lead to the conclusion that the architect of Chartres was uncertain about buttressing. This conclusion is corroborated by the entirely different picture that emerges when one examines the choir at Bourges, built at the same time as Chartres but with light, open buttresses that offer a strong contrast to the heavy, even ponderous, system at Chartres.

THE CHOIR OF BOURGES

In planning the model test to determine the function and effectiveness of the flying buttresses of Bourges, it was necessary to account for its sexpartite vaulting (figure 24). Unlike the quadripartite vaults of Chartres, which distribute equal loads to all the interior piers, sexpartite vaults transmit alternating high and low loadings to primary and secondary piers along the interior aisle.[12] At Bourges the secondary piers are somewhat lighter than the primary piers, but the remainder of the structural system is the same at both primary and secondary sections. Hence it can be assumed that the structure at a primary section is subjected to greater stress than that of a secondary section. For this reason, only the primary section was modeled. This model was tested under both dead-weight loading (plate 3) and simulated wind loads.[13]

Meteorological data similar to those used for the Chartres studies were not available for Bourges. The best data applicable to Bourges were for Chateauroux, some 50 km to the southwest, for a 10-year period. These data indicate that Bourges is in a more sheltered area than Chartres. The maximum mean wind velocity at the elevation of the cathedral roof was calculated as 105 km/hr (65 mph), compared to 135 km/hr (84 mph) for Chartres. Since wind forces on a building are produced as a function of the square of the wind velocity, the calculated maximum total force acting on each bay of the cathedral was only 55,000 kg (120,000 lbs) for Bourges, significantly less than the figure of 100,000 kg (220,000 lbs) at Chartres.

Under the action of combined dead-weight and wind loading, the stress levels throughout the section were found to be quite low. The highest compression stress, at the base of the main piers, was found to be 21 kg/cm² (300 psi), or about two-thirds of the maximum levels usually found in High Gothic buildings. Part of this reduction is attributable to the lower ambient wind speeds, but even more of it is due to the building's lightweight structure and the broader profile of its transverse section. Indeed the findings are mainly attributable to the boldness of the choir's designer.

Since the choir at Bourges has no upper flyer at roof level, the relatively slender, unsupported, main pier extension was scrutinized for possible signs of tensile cracking. It was seen that the thrust of the vault is entirely carried by the lower of the two tiers of flying buttresses that support the clerestory wall. Hence the higher tier of flyers must have been placed to provide support against roof and parapet wind loading. Why were they not brought up close to the roof as were the flyers at Chartres or, for that matter, the seven piers in the nave at Bourges that were constructed after 1232? The answer

24 Bourges Cathedral.
Interior as seen from the
nave.

can be seen in the choir clerestory if one examines the intersection of the higher flying buttress with the pier extension (figure 21). At this point of greatest bending, the pier extension is reinforced by the lower part of the parapet to form a stout T-section. The effectiveness of this combination was demonstrated in the model tests, which revealed that the onset of tensile stress—which occurs in the windward upper pier extension just at the top of the upper flying buttress—does not take place until gusts reach a mean wind velocity at rooftop level of 92 km/hr (57 mph). Even under the most severe wind conditions, tension is less than 17 kg/cm² (10 psi), well below the tensile strength of the mortar.[14]

A quantitative comparison of the effectiveness of the buttressing systems of Chartres and Bourges can now be made. The onset of tensile stress in the nave of Chartres occurs with a rooftop wind velocity of 90 km/hr. The corresponding value for Bourges is 92 km/hr. It can be concluded that the light structure of the choir at Bourges provides a measure of safety that is comparable to that afforded by the much heavier configuration of the nave at Chartres.

Additional light is shed on the achievement of the architect of Bourges by a structural critique of the Late Gothic church of St. Ouen in Rouen published in 1902 by the French architectural authority Julien Guadet (see chapter 7).[15] He proposed a hypothetical alternate design for St. Ouen in which the original interior configuration is unaltered but the buttressing system is considerably lightened by substituting steeply inclined parabolic arches for the Gothic flying buttresses. Besides requiring less material, the alternative design implies a simpler construction process. Guadet included a graphical force analysis, taking into account the effect of gravity loadings to substantiate his design. But that early method of analysis has certain limitations not shared by the photoelastic model method.[16] A model test of Guadet's configuration under grav-

ity loading was performed, and although some further modifications might be necessary if wind forces were taken into account, the test showed his design to be reasonable.[17]

Guadet's alternate design for St. Ouen can be considered a theoretically more advanced Gothic structural form that represents how the form might have evolved if some techniques of scientific analysis had been available to the builders. Hence it is particularly interesting to juxtapose the sections of the three buildings, which are all of similar size, to reveal an obvious hierarchy (figure 25). The great reduction in the amount of materials used for both Bourges and the hypothetical St. Ouen is achieved by carrying the vault and roof forces more directly to the foundations by raising the angle of the flying buttresses and consequently lowering the height of the pier buttresses. With only primitive machinery available for the quarrying, transportation, shaping, and lifting of the huge stones into place, the 60-percent reduction in weight of the pier buttresses at Bourges must have represented a tremendous economy in construction.

It could be argued that the more efficient buttressing of Bourges, with its highly sloped flyers and low pier buttresses, came about because of the necessity to span an additional aisle with the flying buttresses rather than because of the original master's superior understanding of structural design. But this argument is refuted by reviewing the five-aisled churches that were strongly influenced by Bourges—Branner's so-called "school of Bourges"—the abbey of St. Martin at Tours and the cathedrals of Burgos, Le Mans, Toledo, and Coutances, all designed in the second quarter of the thirteenth century. The extant buildings of this group—all except the abbey of St. Martin—show no appreciation of the sophistication of the structure of Bourges and demonstrate that the technical achievement of the original master of

Bourges

Chartres

25 Comparative sections
of Chartres, Bourges, and
Guadet's St. Ouen indi-
cate a design progression
to lighter buttressing.

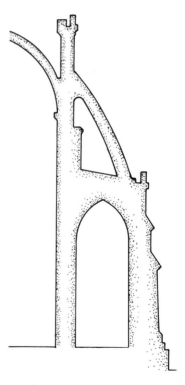

St. Ouen (modified)

Bourges could not just have been the fortuitous result of the solution to a five-aisled building program.[18] For example, the bifurcated array of buttresses supporting the hemicycle (the rounded end portion of the choir) at Le Mans, one of the most visually striking structures of the era (figure 26), can hardly be justified on structural engineering grounds when it is compared with the relatively simple buttress system supporting the even higher hemicycle of Bourges.

The only legitimate structural heir to the Bourges choir is the nave of Bourges itself. Constructed between 1225 and 1255 by the successors of the original master, it deserves closer examination as a member of the "school of Bourges," since it is the only case in which the structural example of the choir of Bourges has been closely followed.

THE NAVE OF BOURGES

The end of the first phase of construction at Bourges is clearly marked on the exterior as one moves from east to west, first, by the enlargement of the flying buttresses and, second, by a change in the window motifs that permits larger areas of glass in the nave clerestory and side aisles. Construction of the nave in the later campaigns is characterized by increases in the height at which the upper flyers abut the pier extensions and by an increase in the size of three of the four flyers (figure 27).[19] The increased height of the abutment of the upper flyers might be explained on the grounds that it would result in much better resistance to roof and parapet wind loading. Yet the choir section had already proved stable without such a change.

Since the principal difference between the original design of the choir at Bourges and the later nave is the progressively more conservative construction of the flying buttress system, model testing of the nave under wind and dead loads would indicate what, if anything, was to be gained by this change. In a second photo-elastic model test,[20] which compared the structural performance of the nave with that of the choir, two important observations resulted. The first demonstrated the inferior structural quality of the design of the nave's system of buttresses compared to that of the choir. The second demonstrated the ability of the modeling technique itself to identify in yet another case highly-localized, critical tensile regions that are verifiable from inspecting the buildings themselves.

Whatever the impetus to increase the height at which the flying buttress abutted the clerestory, the increase was achieved by making both upper flyers deeper in section. The increased stiffness of these flyers is so great that under both dead and wind loading, only low levels of photoelastic activity were observed in the experiments (figure 28, point *a*). Interpretation of the patterns indicates that the material strength of the flyers is greater than is needed for their task.

The section depth of the lower outer flyer was also increased. This second enlargement may have been made solely for visual reasons. The two outer flyers, the visible pair, have been given similar proportions while the inner flyers, the lower of which is not readily visible from the ground, have not been similarly matched. There is some irony here, since it is the lower inner flyers that receive the thrust of the main vault.

At its heaviest, most conservative section, the flying buttresses of the nave employ approximately 60 percent more stone than the flyers of a typical choir section. In addition, the heavier nave section required passage openings for access to the roof through the intermediate pier buttresses that were unnecessary in the choir (plate 4).[21] The model analysis shows the intermediate pier buttresses to be free of tensile stresses under combined wind and dead loads below the first side aisle vault. Above the vault, though, the passages so weakened the fabric that a

26 Le Mans Cathedral.
Choir buttressing is the
most elaborate of the era.

27 Bourges. Clerestory
buttressing viewed from
the northwest tower.
Note the increase in size
of the later, western
flying buttresses
(foreground).

combined wind- and dead-load tensile stress of approximately 4 kg/cm² (57 psi) developed on the outer segment of the intermediate pier buttresses next to the passageway (figure 28, point b).

The model's prediction of tensile stress was verified by examining the existing fabric of Bourges, which reveals the systematic replacement of the stone on the outside of these passages. The new stone is evident in plate 4 (this photograph was taken in 1971). It can be concluded, then, that even the enlargement of the flying buttresses in the nave, in comparison with those of the choir, could not ensure a more reliable structure. This change, in fact, produced problem areas that were not present in the original design.

One can speculate that a second Bourges architect, who clearly attempted to maintain the visual pattern of the choir buttresses when he designed the nave, was uneasy over his predecessor's daring because of his own familiarity with the structure of Chartres. He modified the original design by deepening the flying buttresses and raising the point of abutment of the higher buttress against the pier extension. Yet in doing so, he gave up some material economies of the original design for no significant gains in structural performance.

Thus, although Chartres made a major aesthetic contribution by becoming the model for the great High Gothic buildings that followed it, the model analyses have shown that, where technical matters are concerned, the cathedral's design was far less revolutionary than has been claimed. On the other hand, the analyses have also shown that the original structural solution at Bourges was unique. Even so, its full significance was not appreciated until late in the Gothic era when its steep, sloping buttresses reappeared in several large churches, including the choir of the parish church of Saint-Étienne at Beauvais and the nave of Bath Cathedral.

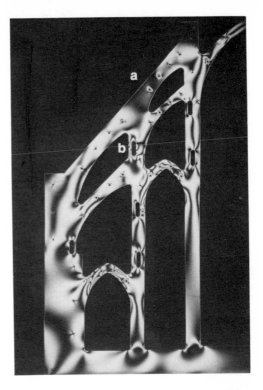

28 Bourges nave model. Photoelastic interference pattern produced by simulated wind loading.

NOTES

Material for this chapter was derived from Robert Mark, "The Structural Analysis of Gothic Cathedrals" (see note 13); Alan Borg and Robert Mark, "Chartres Cathedral: A Reinterpretation of its Structure" (see note 9); and from Maury I. Wolfe and Robert Mark, "Gothic Cathedral Buttressing: The Experiment at Bourges and its Influence" (see note 18). The most comprehensive writing on Bourges is Robert Branner's *La cathédrale de Bourges et sa place dans l'architecture Gothique* (see note 3). For the structure of Chartres, see John James, *Chartres les constructeurs* (see note 1).

1 The nave of Chartres, which embodies heavier flying buttresses than the choir, is generally (but by no means universally) assumed to be of earlier design than the choir and therefore more contemporaneous in design with Bourges. On the basis of recent archaeological research, John James infers that construction proceeded in horizontal layers across the entire building (*Chartres les constructeurs* [Chartres: Société Archéologique d'Eure-et-Loir, 1977], pp. 27ff.)

2 Jean Bony, "The Resistance to Chartres in Thirteenth-century Architecture," *Journal of the British Archaeological Association* XX–XXI (1957–1958):35–52.

3 Robert Branner, *La cathédrale de Bourges et sa place dans l'architecture Gothique* (Paris/Bourges: Éditions Tardy, 1962).

4 The names of the designers of both of these monuments have been lost to history, and there is the possibility that more than one master was responsible. James (*Chartres*) goes so far as to cite forty different building campaigns at Chartres under the direction of almost as many masters.

5 Paul Frankl, *Gothic Architecture* (Harmondsworth, England: Penguin Books, 1962), p. 79.

6 George Henderson, *Chartres* (Harmondsworth, England: Penguin Books, 1968), p. 111.

7 Otto von Simson, *The Gothic Cathedral* (New York: Harper, 1956), p. 204.

8 Eugène E. Viollet-le-Duc, *Dictionnaire raisonné de l'architecture française du XIe au XVIe siècle*, 10 vols. (Paris: Librairies-Imprimeries Réunies, 1854–1868), I, p. 65.

9 Alan Borg and Robert Mark, "Chartres Cathedral: A Reinterpretation of its Structure," *Art Bulletin* LV (September 1973):367–372.

10 The modeled section, at a scale of 1:180, was taken from a reproduction of a drawing by Robert Branner (*Chartres Cathedral* [New York: Norton, 1969], figure 14). Wind-loading information for Chartres was based on Paris data. A maximum velocity of 135 km/hr (84 mph) was assumed at the roof tip, 51 m (167 ft) above ground level. Model loadings were applied at a scale of 1:75,000. The ratio of the breadth of the upper flyers to the breadth of the lower flyers in the nave was maintained in the model.

11 A number of similar instances when prior modeling led to the disclosure of tensile distress or repairs necessitated by tension in the building fabric are reported throughout the text. These are summarized in chapter 9.

12 See section on sexpartite vaults in chapter 8.

13 The 1:107 scale modeled section is from Branner, *La cathédrale de Bourges*. Dead loads for the choir of Bourges were modeled at a scale of 1:148,000; wind loads at a scale of 1:100,000. The twin pinnacles on the pier buttresses, illustrated in figure 21, were not taken into account, as these were added for appearance in the nineteenth century. Photoelastic patterns for the choir under wind loads have been published in Robert Mark, "The Structural Analysis of Gothic Cathedrals," *Scientific American* 227 (November 1972):90–99.

14 The analysis also indicated that, without pinnacles, the lower pier buttress of Bourges would not be subjected to tension; the existing pinnacles have no structural role as they do, for example, on the Amiens pier buttress (see chapter 4).

15 Julien Guadet, *Éléments et théorie de l'architecture*, 3 vols. (Paris: Librairie de la Construction Moderne, 1909), III, pp. 340–349.

16 With the graphical-statical method, the interaction between the structural members cannot be taken into account. For example, in the actual structure, any deflection of the pier extension at its intersection with the arch must be accompanied by a corresponding deflection of the end of the arch. Considerable forces can be set up by these interactions.

17 Robert Mark, "The Church of St. Ouen, Rouen: A Reexamination of Gothic Structure," *American Scientist* 56 (1968):390–399.

18 Maury I. Wolfe and Robert Mark, "Gothic Cathedral Buttressing: The Experiment at Bourges and its Influence," *Journal of the Society of Architectural Historians* XXXIII (1974): 17–26.

19 These series of increases are not symmetric on the north and south sides of the cathedral. The historical import of this asymmetry is not clear, since some of the vaults at the west end of the nave were reconstructed after the north tower collapsed in 1506. See Branner, *La cathédrale de Bourges,* p. 71.

20 The second model approximates a section through the heaviest, westernmost bays. The model section was assumed to be through a primary pier, carrying the greater load, and scaled to 1:107. Dead loads were modeled at a scale of 1:72,000. The wind load, assumed to be the same as that on a choir bay, was modeled at a scale of 1:50,500. The model dimensions were established using a small section drawing from Amédée Boivet, *La cathédrale de Bourges,* Petites Monographies des Grands Édifices de la France (Paris: Henri Laurens, n.d.), p. 59, interpolations from Branner's drawing of the choir (*La cathédrale de Bourges*), and estimates from my own observations. The model ignores the existence of overvaulting (transverse walls above the vaults) at some of the nave sections.

21 The intermediate pier buttresses at Bourges, which support the center of the flying buttress system, maintain a relatively low profile both because of the steepness of the flyers and the great height of the first side aisles. At Le Mans and Beauvais the intermediate pier buttresses have the form of tall slender shafts (cf. figure 26, plate 4, and figure 43).

4

QUINTESSENTIAL HIGH GOTHIC: AMIENS CATHEDRAL AND MEDIEVAL ENGINEERING

The cathedral of Amiens (figure 29), begun in 1220, is generally considered to be the summa of French High Gothic.[1] More information has come down to us about the masters responsible for the design of this cathedral than about the designers of many earlier medieval buildings. The first was Robert de Luzarches. He set the course of the overall design, and under his direction the nave was completed by about 1233. In contrast to the usual practice of constructing the choir and then the nave, Amiens was built from west to east. The vaults of the choir were not in place until 1269, and by then the earlier High Gothic pattern had been superseded by the newer Rayonnant style.[2]

It is the earlier nave configuration of Amiens that historians most frequently consider as representative of the High Gothic ideal of illumination and structural display. Amiens has been chosen for this tribute both because of the relative lightness of its structure and the restrained elegance of its decoration and because it is the largest of the French cathedrals that have survived totally intact—without any taint of the collapse of the only French cathedral to exceed its 42-m (138-ft) vaulting height, Beauvais. The choice of the nave of Amiens may also be based on the availability of the frequently reproduced drawing by Viollet-le-Duc (figure 11) and his comparison of Amiens, as representative of High Gothic, with classical proportional systems.[3]

This chapter will discuss some of the results of the application of photoelastic modeling to this quintessential example of the High Gothic style and will both contribute new evidence to a long-standing debate on the structural function of a characteristic Gothic architectural element, the pinnacle, and offer new insights into medieval structural design.

29 Amiens Cathedral
from the west.

THE PINNACLE

Of all Viollet-le-Duc's arguments for the rationality of Gothic architecture, none has seemed more tenuous than his claim that the pinnacles (see, for example, plate 5), placed upon the pier buttresses, help to maintain structural integrity. His persistent critic, Pol Abraham, found major flaws in Viollet-le-Duc's assumption, pointing out that one must discriminate between the various uses of the pinnacle. According to Abraham, the pinnacle could be useful: it augmented the stability of a pier buttress if a vertical line taken through its center passed through the buttress's center of gravity. But the pinnacle could also be detrimental. Generally speaking, if the pinnacle were constructed too close to the external edge of the pier buttress, the buttress's stability would be diminished. Pointing out that many pinnacles were indeed constructed near the outer edge of pier buttresses, Abraham asserted that the practical application of Viollet-le-Duc's theory that pinnacles augmented stability must sometimes have had the reverse of the desired effect. Moreover the influence of the pinnacles could also be negligible because their weight was so small compared to the enormous weight of the pier buttress itself. Finally, Abraham pointed out that many buildings constructed from the beginning of the Gothic period to the end of the third quarter of the thirteenth century had no pinnacles at all.[4]

Abraham's argument is sensible, and his point that one must look at each use of the pinnacle individually is well taken. But his thesis is weakened by the fact that it does not cover all of the possible functions of a pinnacle. For instance, the weight of a pinnacle can provide additional compressive forces to the stones below it to further consolidate them and thereby help to prevent their lateral sliding, or shearing, under the action of thrust from the flying buttress. This function, moreover, does not depend on the exact position of the pinnacle on the pier buttress. While

this fact does not contradict Abraham's observation about stability, it does throw a positive light on pinnacles, even those located near the outer edge of the pier buttress.

These contrary views, and the fact that Abraham cited Amiens as one of the major buildings in which the pinnacle was incorrectly located, led to a model analysis of the cathedral nave that was designed to examine the function of the pinnacle.

The nave section as it was originally constructed (figure 30) provided the basis of the model configuration. The model was tested under wind loading and under a simulated dead weight that did not include the weight of the pinnacle. This was taken into account analytically at a later stage.[5] (A photograph of the wind-loaded model appears in figure 16, and the resulting photoelastic interference pattern is shown in figure 31.)

When the results of both tests were superimposed, only a few local regions of tension were noted: at the ends of the flying buttress and, significantly, along the outer edge of the pier buttress, particularly near the pinnacle of the leeward rather than the windward side of the nave. Figure 32 shows the force distributions in this region of the structure under the action of wind alone; wind and dead weight without the pinnacle; and wind and dead weight with the weight of the pinnacle taken into account. The results show that in the absence of the pinnacle, the pier buttress is subjected to tension under the loading of both wind and dead weight, whereas the addition of the pinnacle on its outer edge brings it into a state of compression. One may infer, therefore, that the presence of the pinnacle on the outer edge of the buttress had the effect of canceling local tension that, in its absence, would have occurred under high wind conditions.

Tests were also made to see what effect the pinnacle would have if it were placed on the inside edge of the pier buttress. The results indicated that even

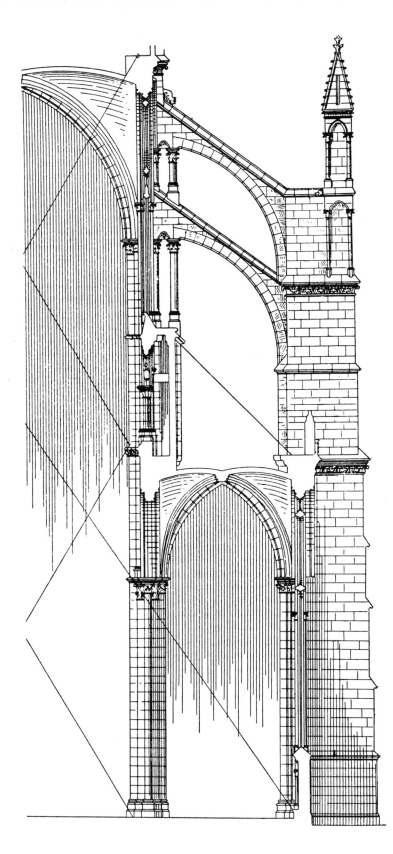

30 Amiens Cathedral.
Section of the thirteenth-
century nave from Georg
Gottfried Dehio and
G. von Bezold, *Die
Kirchliche Baukunst des
Abendlandes* (Stüttgart:
Hildesheim, 1892–1901;
reissued, 1969).

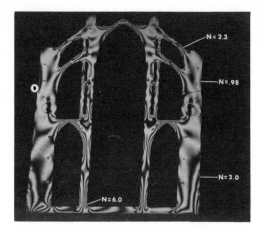

31 Photoelastic interference pattern in the nave section of Amiens under simulated wind loading. Interference orders (N) are noted.

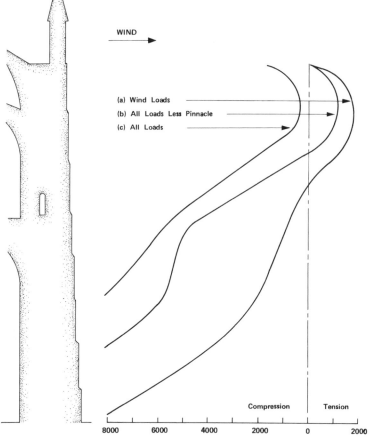

WIND

(a) Wind Loads
(b) All Loads Less Pinnacle
(c) All Loads

Compression   Tension

8000   6000   4000   2000   0   2000

Force (lb./in.)

32 Force distributions along the outer edge of Amiens pier buttress. The effect of the pinnacle is to shift the entire force distribution into the compression region.

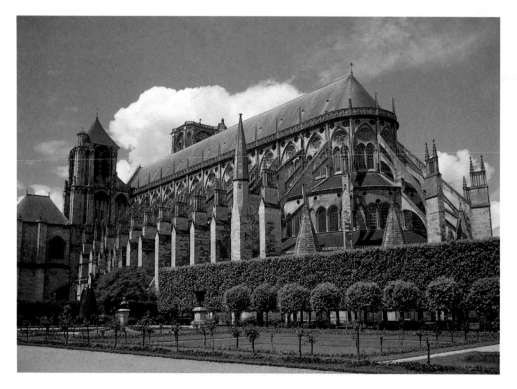

1 Bourges Cathedral from
the southeast. Con-
struction of the choir
began in 1195, when ex-
posed flying buttresses
were a relatively new
device. In contrast to the
massive buttressing sys-
tem of Chartres Cathe-
dral, the flyers of Bourges
are light and steeply
sloped.

2 Detail of Chartres
Cathedral nave model
with upper flyers. Photo-
elastic interference
pattern produced by
simulated wind loadings.
Each color represents a
different magnitude of
force intensity. Photo
by Sepp Seitz.

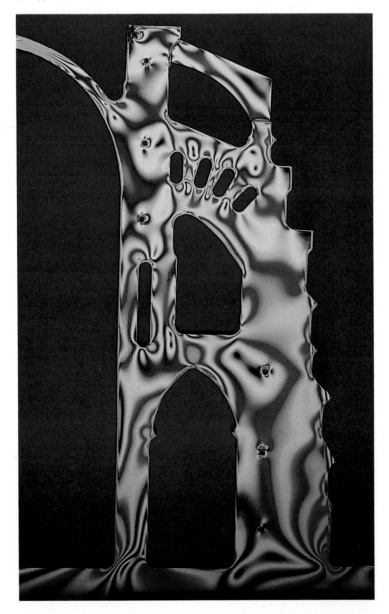

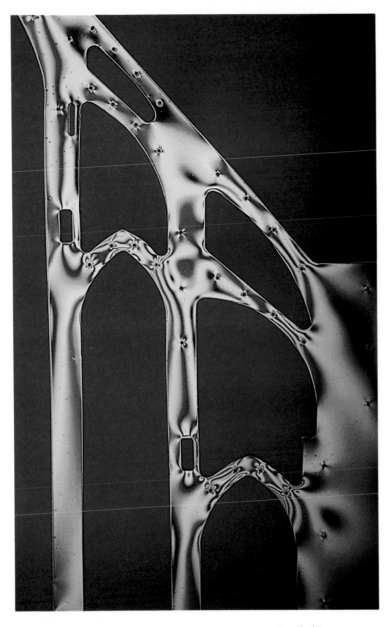

3 Detail of Bourges
Cathedral choir model.
Photoelastic interference
pattern produced by
simulated dead-weight
loading. Photo by
Sepp Seitz.

4 Passageway in inter-
mediate pier buttress of
Bourges Cathedral nave.
Replaced stone along the
exterior of buttresses
at openings confirmed the
predictions of local ten-
sile stress from the model
analysis.

5 Pinnacles on the pier
buttresses of the nave of
Amiens Cathedral. Re-
sults of photoelastic
modeling show that the
presence of the pinnacles
on the outer edge of these
buttresses help to main-
tain structural integrity
by producing local
compressive forces.

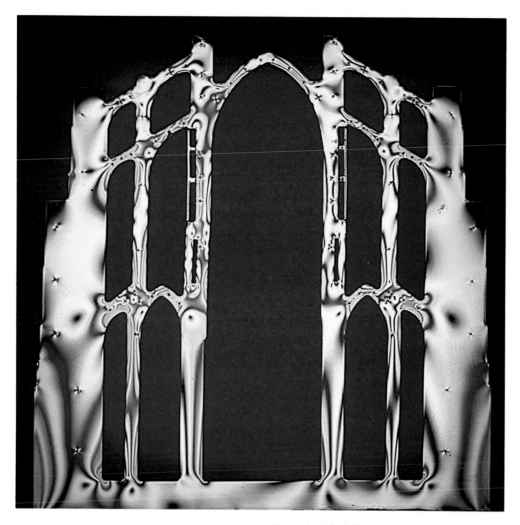

6 Beauvais Cathedral
choir model. Photoelastic
interference pattern
produced by simulated
wind loading.

7 Amiens Cathedral.
Quadripartite vaulting
of the south transept is
typical of that used in
French High Gothic
churches. Photo by Allen
Hess. Separation courtesy
of Polaroid Corporation.

8 Sexpartite vaulting
of the nave of Bourges
Cathedral. Modeling
shows that ribs have no
more structural impor-
tance in sexpartite vaulting than they do in
quadripartite vaulting.

9 View of the cathedral
of Palma, Majorca, from
the harbor. The mas-
sive pier buttresses are a
departure from the
French High Gothic. The
lower tier of buttresses
supports the walls of
chapels set within the
bays. Photo by M. Dean.

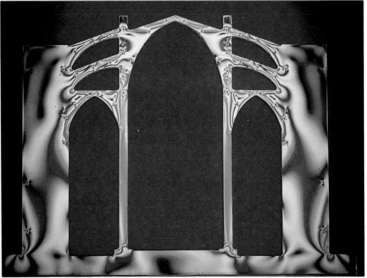

10 Cathedral of Palma,
Majorca, nave model.
Photoelastic interference
pattern produced by
simulated dead-weight
loading. The almost uni-
form color in the main
piers indicates a negli-
gible amount of bending.

in calm air the pinnacle in this position acted to produce tension along the outside edge of the buttress.[6] From all of this information, it is possible to conclude that the pinnacle at Amiens acts as a prestressing element that prevents tension in the pier buttress.

It is also clear from these results that both Viollet-le-Duc and Abraham in part misunderstood the role of the pinnacle. Viollet-le-Duc, while he viewed the extra weight of the pinnacle on the pier buttress as advantageous, did not discriminate about its placement. Abraham's analysis, while more rigorous, did not take into account the role of the pinnacle in preventing pier buttress shearing. More important, Abraham did not detect the much more subtle role of the pinnacle in helping to prevent local tension.

HIGH GOTHIC DESIGN

The detailed study of the nave at Amiens afforded a vantage point from which to make some fresh general observations about the design of High Gothic buildings. One of these concerned the influence of high winds in determining buttress configuration. As the height of churches increased near the close of the twelfth century, wind action became an even more important factor in structural design. In addition to having larger lateral surfaces at higher elevations, the taller buildings were also subjected to higher average wind velocities. These buildings, therefore, had to withstand far greater lateral forces than their lower predecessors, and this is reflected in the buttress systems of almost all the major Gothic churches.

To maintain the stability of the upper clerestory, a second tier of flying buttresses was placed above the tier designed to resist the thrust of the vault. As Fitchen has noted, there has been some dispute among architectural historians over the role of the upper flying buttress.[7] However, any doubts about its structural function were dispelled by the results of the photoelastic model tests of Amiens. These results showed that under dead-weight loading alone the upper flying buttress was subjected to low compression forces and, in effect, supported merely its own weight. But when wind forces were applied, the upper flying buttress was seen in the wind-loading photoelastic pattern (figure 31) to resist almost entirely the high wind loadings acting on the roof and on the upper clerestory. The upper flying buttress, properly designed, therefore had a vital structural function in stabilizing the upper clerestory and the high timber roofs of buildings such as the cathedral of Amiens.

As noted, the model tests also revealed that the ends of the flying buttresses displayed symptoms of tension. Although this tension only occurred under magnitudes of wind forces that are encountered only rarely in a structure's lifetime, it points to a weakness prevalent in many Gothic churches. The alternation in the buttress of compression in quiescent wind conditions and tension caused by bending under high wind gusts against both sides of the building causes cyclic racking of the mortar. This action creates crevices in the mortar in which ice can form. Both alternating stress and the formation of ice contribute to the deterioration of the ends of the flying buttresses, which need periodic maintenance at much more frequent intervals than is necessary in other parts of the building fabric.

The model tests also throw additional light on the levels of compressive stress found in High Gothic churches. The location of highest compressive stress in the nave at Amiens under dead-weight loading alone, 19 kg/cm^2 (270 psi), is at the inside edge of the piers just above the footing. When wind load is added, giving a total maximum wind- and dead-load stress of 34 kg/cm^2 (480 psi) the location of highest compressive stress remains the same. These moderate levels of compressive stress have been found to be typical for extant High Gothic churches and are, no doubt, a factor in their long life.

A further observation, and probably one of the most significant that resulted from all the technical studies of Gothic building, concerns the identification of a possible Gothic experimental design method. We stand in awe of the ingenuity of the Gothic architects, particularly when we consider that even Galileo, centuries later, did not correctly describe bending stress distributions in a simple beam.[8] How, then, can we explain the sophistication of the placement of the Amiens pinnacle so that it prestressed the outside edge of the pier buttress?

My work with small-scale models to analyze the behavior of full-scale buildings led me to speculate on whether the medieval builder had available an experimental method parallel to mine, using the full-scale building as his experimental model. It seemed to me that he did. Since cathedrals were built over long periods of time, tensile cracking, caused either by high winds or by the removal of temporary construction supports, could have been readily observed in the newly-set, weak lime mortar between the stones of the bays constructed first. As a result, changes would have been made in later bays to eliminate the cause of the cracking. These successive modifications could then have been the source of structural innovation, with the pinnacle on the pier buttress of Amiens as an outstanding example.

It is interesting to speculate how this full-scale experimental technique might have been used to rectify other pitfalls in Gothic design. For example, the tensile cracking of the mortar at the ends of the flying buttress must have been just as evident to the medieval builder as it is to restorers today. However, the solution for reducing bending at the ends of the flying buttress is not as obvious as the prevention of tensile cracking at the top of the outer edge of the pier buttress by placing additional stone at that point. From studying the choir at Bourges we know that the bending can be reduced by increasing the slope of the flying buttress, but the medieval designer either did not recognize the Bourges solution or he did not wish to alter the appearance of the classic High Gothic structure with its very tall pier buttresses and relatively horizontal flyers. The study of the choir vaults at Beauvais, discussed in the next chapter, demonstrates that the collapse of a major building might well have been avoided if cracking in mortar, caused by tension, had been observed in time. In this case, however, the critical region of the structure was enclosed by a timber roof and was not readily accessible for inspection.

The results of these studies of the structure of Amiens Cathedral, based on photoelastic modeling, indicate that the analysis has much to offer. For the architectural historian, it can bring fresh evidence to arguments based on insufficient technical information. For the historian of science, it brings new insights into the genius of the Gothic master builders who raised such impressive monuments to their faith in the near-total absence of structural theory. And, not least of all, it may explain to the keepers of the fabric of Gothic churches why they must so constantly replace and repair the stones of one or another particular area in their historic charges.

NOTES

Material for this chapter was derived from Robert Mark and Richard Alan Prentke, "Model Analysis of Gothic Structure" (see note 6); and from Robert Mark and Ronald S. Jonash, "Wind Loading on Gothic Structure," *Journal of the Society of Architectural Historians* XXIX (October 1970):222–230. The most comprehensive description of the fabric of Amiens is George Durand, *Monographie de l'église Nôtre-Dame, Cathédrale d'Amiens* (Paris: Librairie A. Picard et Fils, 1901–1903).

1 See, for example, Whitney S. Stoddard, *Monastery and Cathedral in France* (Middletown, Conn.: Wesleyan University Press, 1966), p. 217.

2 Note that this stylistic change followed by a short period a modification of the structural design. The original triforium passage was blind because the outer wall beyond it was covered by a timber side aisle roof. The roof in turn was partially supported by the transverse walls placed above the side aisle vaults to help to brace the lower portion of the clerestory. At the beginning of the thirteenth century, as the role of the flying buttress seems to have become better understood, these transverse walls were dispensed with, although the form of the side aisle roof remained unchanged (see figure 1 and compare Laon and Reims). It was not until Thomas de Cormont, the second master at Amiens, recognized that the side aisle roof could now be divided into pyramidal sections that light was admitted at the triforium level.

3 Eugène E. Viollet-le-Duc, *Entretiens sur l'architecture*, 2 vols. (Paris: A. Morel, 1863–1872), I, pp. 330ff.

4 Pol Abraham, *Viollet-le-Duc et le Rationalisme Médiéval* (Paris: Vincent, Fréal & Cie., 1934), pp. 88ff.

5 A 1:136 scale model, fabricated from 1.0-cm (.40-in) thick cast epoxy, was used. It was tested under simulated dead weight at a load-scale factor of 1:110,000 and under wind loadings at a 1:135,000 scale. Wind velocity data and some further details of the Amiens modeling are described in chapter 2 along with assumptions incorporated into the model. Two additional assumptions were that the walls over the transverse arches of the side aisles were considered to be structural and were therefore included in the model; and, for simplicity, that the colonnettes beneath the flying buttresses were modeled with monolithic end-attachments.

The footings at Amiens are of particular importance to the model analyses because they are the basis for the assumption that the pier bases were fully fixed against any forces tending to displace them. The area below the pier buttresses was excavated in the nineteenth century. (See Eugène E. Viollet-le-Duc, *Dictionnaire raisonné de l'architecture française du XIe au XVIe siècle*, 10 vols. [Paris: Librairies-Imprimeries Réunies, 1854–1868], IV, p. 175). The footings of the cathedral extend 8 m (26 ft) below ground level. The first three courses of stone below ground are of extremely hard and well-faced sandstone, as are the adjacent six courses above ground. Supporting these is a single course of stone from Croissy, followed by fourteen courses of a mixture of chalk and silica cut in large pieces 30 cm to 40 cm (12 to 16 in) thick, from the quarries of Blavelincourt, near Amiens. A bed of concrete about 40 cm thick is laid below this. Below the concrete is a 40-cm layer of clay resting on the natural clay of the ground. Behind the facings of the footing is a conglomeration of large fragments of silex stone in a hard mortar.

6 Robert Mark and Richard Alan Prentke, "Model Analysis of Gothic Structure," *Journal of the Society of Architectural Historians* XXVII (1968):44–48.

7 John Fitchen, "A Comment on the Function of the Upper Flying Buttress in French Gothic Architecture," *Gazette des Beaux Arts*, series 6, XLV (February 1955):69–90.

8 Galileo's erroneous distribution is discussed in Stephen P. Timoshenko, *History of Strength of Materials* (New York: McGraw-Hill, 1953), pp. 12–13.

5

THE COLLAPSE OF BEAUVAIS CATHEDRAL

Major interest in Beauvais Cathedral (figure 33) has centered on the height of its vaults, 48 m (158 ft), and their collapse in 1284. Indeed, Robert Branner lamented that "the general admiration of Beauvais has been stimulated by a venture that was a tour-de-force, and an unsuccessful one at that, while the profoundly original stylistic part of the monument has been all but ignored."[1] Yet, in spite of the fascination with the collapse of the high vaults, the cause of the failure has never been adequately explained.

Beauvais was begun in 1225 by an unknown first master whose construction was concluded before 1245, by which time the choir below the main triforium was complete. A second master may have worked for a short period on the piers and vaults of the transept aisles, and from about 1250 or 1255, a third master took over the work and carried on until 1272, erecting the high choir vaults and buttressing. Figures 34, 35, and 36 show, respectively, reconstructions of the original plan for the whole building by Viollet-le-Duc, the interior of the original choir by Branner, and the cross section of the original northern half of the easternmost straight bay in the choir by the nineteenth-century architect, Benouville.

In 1284, all or part of the high vaults over the original three straight bays of the choir collapsed. Repairs, completed by about 1337, included replacement of all the original quadripartite vaults by sexpartite vaults and the erection of extra, unbuttressed piers in the three bays. Work ceased during the Hundred Years War, and the completion of the transept was not begun until about 1500.

Between 1564 and 1569, before work on the nave was far advanced, a gigantic stone tower of some 150 m (490 ft) in height was erected over the crossing. In 1573 the tower collapsed. Damage from this disaster was repaired by 1578, although the tower itself was not replaced. No further major construction was undertaken after that date, leaving the cathedral in its present truncated condition (see

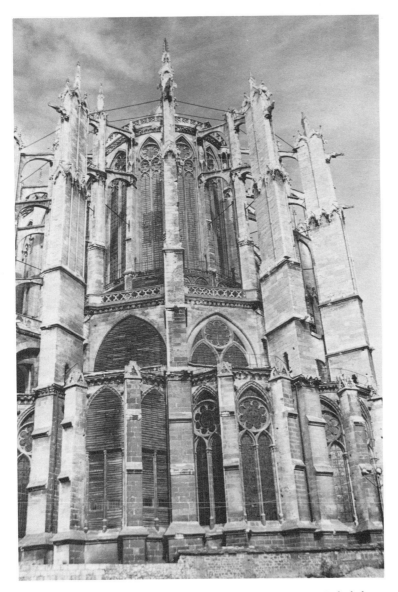

33 Beauvais Cathedral.
View of the hemicycle.
Iron bars are reputed to be
part of the fourteenth-
century reconstruction.

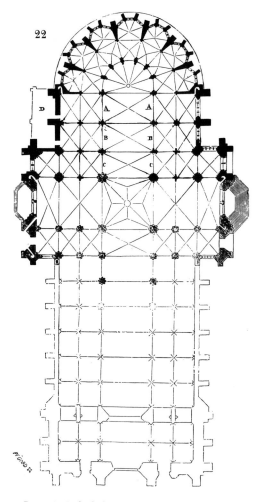

34 Beauvais Cathedral
plan. Reconstruction,
showing unexecuted
nave, by Viollet-le-Duc.
The structure indicated
by the darkened region
was complete in 1272.

figure 34). A cross section of the existing southern half of the easternmost straight bay is shown in figure 37.[2]

Sixteenth-century accounts of the collapse of the tower and the recommendations of contemporary masons about how to prevent its fall make it clear that the two western piers in the crossing failed from progressive movement in a westerly direction because they received insufficient lateral support from the incomplete nave. In contrast to the tower debacle, which is well documented, there are no contemporary accounts of the collapse of the choir's high vaults three centuries earlier. Indeed, as Branner has noted, the entire bibliography on Beauvais is slight for a building of its importance.

THEORIES CONCERNING THE FAILURE

In the absence of any evidence to suggest that the failure of the choir vaults in 1284 was due to some rare, excessive load on the structure such as an earthquake, there is a wide range of speculation about the cause of the collapse. One view is that the high vaults touched the limits of construction in stone. Viollet-le-Duc remarked that "the final limit at which construction of the great churches of the thirteenth century could arrive had been reached in the Beauvais structural system."[3] But, as will become apparent from our further investigations, there is no intrinsic structural principle that would hold Gothic bay construction to a height of 50 meters.

Paul Frankl's comment that the collapse was a failure "not of the architect as artist . . . but of the architect as engineer" is more plausible. Frankl suggests that the structural problem was due to inadequate foundations.[4] However, although differential foundation settlement is often the cause of severe structural damage to buildings,[5] there are no signs of any major deformity caused by settlement in the existing building fabric at Beauvais. Also, since the cathedral was founded on the site

35 Sketch of the original Beauvais choir, derived from archaeological evidence, by Branner.

COUPE

RESTAUREE

36 Beauvais Cathedral
cross section. Recon-
struction showing
northern half of the easternmost straight bay,
viewed from the east,
by Benouville.

of an earlier building and within the walls of the old Roman precinct, it was less likely to have suffered from problems of settlement than major construction begun on fresh ground. The fact that the foundations were by the first Beauvais architect, whose masonry was evidently of higher quality than that of the master of the upper fabric, further weakens Frankl's suggestion.[6]

In the remaining theories, including the hypothesis presented here, the common idea is that there must have been some error in the design of the structure. These include the statements of nineteenth- and twentieth-century commentators who blame the failure on excessively large spans between piers that were too slender in relation to their height and the loads they had to carry.[7] According to this view, the change to sexpartite vaulting and the insertion of additional piers after the collapse of the vaults could have been an attempt to relieve the loads on the original piers. Branner's belief that the vaults were higher than intended by the first master may serve to give further support to this concept. No one, however, has produced a scientific analysis showing that the piers would have buckled under the loading from the original quadripartite vaults, and my own buckling calculation convinced me that the piers were in no such danger.[8]

Jacques Heyman, an engineer at Cambridge University, analyzed the Beauvais structural configuration for stability and concluded that "the fabric of Beauvais in 1272 seems to have been, in the large, almost perfectly designed to fulfill its function" and, hence, the explanation for the collapse had to be sought in some structural detail.[9] Heyman went on to endorse Viollet-le-Duc's theory of failure, which located the fault in the twin colonnettes below the lower tier of flying buttresses (letter A, figure 38). In Viollet-le-Duc's words,

37 Beauvais Cathedral cross section. Southern half of the existing easternmost straight bay, by Corroyer.

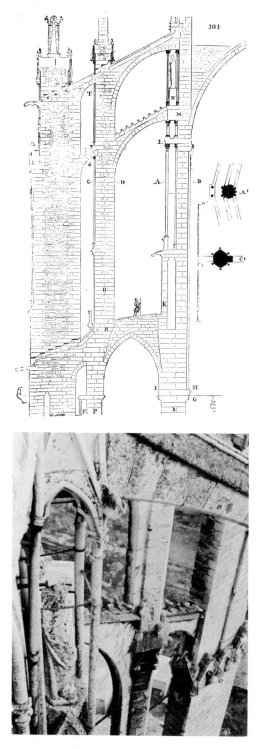

[Beauvais] would have kept perfect stability if the architect had made the two pillars above the triforium stronger and more resistant; if he could have made them from cast iron, for instance. The disorders which have occurred in the structure have all come from this; these [monolithic] columns, too slender, have given way, for they could not resist the weight brought upon them when the inner piers began to settle in consequence of the drying of the mortar [of the coursed construction]. In the disorder, the lintels L [figure 38] were broken and the large blocks M, in swaying, rested too heavily upon the top of the first flying-buttress; this latter was deformed and, the vault following the movement, the pressure upon these flying-buttresses was such that they nearly all were forced outward and their action annulled. In consequence, the upper flying-buttresses were loosened somewhat, since the vault no longer pressed against them. The equilibrium was broken. . . .[10]

Even if it was true that the slender colonnettes buckled and failed by bearing the principal roof and vaulting dead loads, Viollet's explanation, endorsed by Heyman, is open to objection. First, it is crucial to this theory that the twin colonnettes supporting the statues were present in the original construction, prior to 1284. There is no doubt that the statues existed at that date, since they can still be seen on the easternmost choir bay and all around the hemicycle (figure 39). The absence of the statues and the presence of sexpartite vaulting, inserted piers (cf. figures 40 and 35), blocked lower clerestory window heads, and changed mullions and tracery details are the major archaeological evidence that the collapse was confined to the straight bays of the choir and that the easternmost bay is as a result substantially closer to the original state of the choir structure in 1272 than other portions of the straight bays. Evidence for the existence of the twin colonnettes in the thirteenth century is, however, far less convincing.

38 Cross section of the Beauvais hemicycle, by Viollet-le-Duc. In his text, Viollet-le-Duc implied the wall details were similar for the original bays of the choir.

39 Beauvais Cathedral. Statue on hemicycle pier extension.

40 Beauvais Cathedral
choir after 1337 showing
sexpartite vaulting. Photo
by R. Branner.

41 Beauvais Cathedral.
Hemicycle pier extensions
seen from the roof of the
ambulatory.

At present, all of the pier extensions, original and added, are solid masonry at clerestory level, except for the passage openings (figure 41). Viollet-le-Duc stated that one could still recognize the position and approximate the diameters of the twin colonnettes, but it does not seem possible that he could have seen the lower sockets or supports of the colonnettes, since those lower, exterior areas were covered by masonry.[11] If his inference was drawn from the carved blocks on which the statues stand and which receive the ends of the lower flyers, as seen in figure 41 and in his drawing (figure 42), then it is important to note the differences between these lower blocks and the ones above the statues. In the lower block, the trefoil is only a surface relief, and the block remains substantially solid; in the upper block the trefoil is fully pierced as part of a gabled canopy. Viollet-le-Duc's drawing is incorrect in that it shows the lower side of the upper flyer filling the canopy opening. In reality, the flyer abuts the canopy at a higher point (cf. figures 39 and 42). The motif on the surface-carved trefoil also is found on the intermediate pier buttresses that support the center of the flying buttresses and on the exterior pier buttresses (figure 43). On these buttresses, the surface-carved trefoils do receive monolithic colonnettes, but these colonnettes are not the sole support of the masonry above them. They are, rather, merely decorative elements.[12] Had these lower colonnettes been like the upper ones, then the trefoil surmounting them would have been more likely to have been carved through in the manner of the trefoil surmounting the upper colonnettes.

Benouville supports Viollet-le-Duc's theory by adducing as archaeological evidence for the existence of the colonnettes in the thirteenth century the fact that the solid exterior masonry of all the original wall buttresses is not bedded into the wall and is hence an obvious addition (figure 41). However, the only safe conclusion to be drawn from this observation

42 Beauvais Cathedral. Detail of statue on pier extension, by Viollet-le-Duc.

43 Beauvais Cathedral
intermediate pier buttress
on the north side of the
easternmost straight bay.
The upper portion of
this buttress, with its
attached shafts, appears
to be part of the origi-
nal construction. The
lower portion is heavily
reinforced, especially
in the plane correspond-
ing to the direction of
thrusts from the flying
buttresses.

today is that, while all the original wall buttresses in the choir were altered, their original form is still unknown.

Even if it were granted speculatively that the original section was accurately depicted by Viollet-le-Duc, it is still not clear that the failure he describes would have occurred. If the long colonnettes had broken, it is not obvious that the weight of the statue would have been sufficient to displace or significantly rotate the block below it. As shown in Viollet-le-Duc's drawing of a hemicycle section (figure 38), the block M was bedded into the wall. It was also the stone through which the horizontal vault thrust was transmitted to the lower flyer. This horizontal force on the block would have increased its frictional resistance to displacement by the weight of the statue.

The process that Viollet-le-Duc put forward as having caused the breaking of the colonnettes is also suspect. In his account the coursed section of the pier extension settled relative to the monolithic colonnettes because of shrinkage caused by drying of the mortar. From what is known of the behavior of medieval mortar and the nature of its construction, it is extremely unlikely that differential movement of the type described could have displaced sufficient load from the wall proper onto the colonnettes to break them after twelve years. Initial shrinkage of a lime mortar during setting could not have produced the dimensional change required by Viollet-le-Duc's account of the collapse because this initial dimensional change would have occurred in the course of construction and long before any vault loads were imposed.[13]

If we further allow that during the 30-year period from the beginning of the upper work at Beauvais to the collapse of 1284 all of the mortar within the pier extensions became carbonated, it still does not follow that the shrinkage associated with carbonation would have been sufficient to produce the dimensional change required to overload the colonnettes.[14] Using the very conservative assumption that the mortar joints make up 10 percent of the total height of the ashlar exterior of the pier extensions, a simple calculation shows that the carbonation shrinkage along the 11-m (36-ft) section of the pier extension adjacent to the colonnettes would be too small to endanger them as Viollet-le-Duc imagined: the largest ratio of dimensional change that could be expected is 0.0001, an amount approximately half that of the strain that would need to be produced before the colonnettes received a load sufficient to buckle them.

The one other mechanism by which dimensional change could occur is creep, the unrecoverable viscous flow of materials under load. Masonry construction may exhibit creep in the mortar whether or not the masonry blocks themselves are subject to creep. This deformation, although usually small, can be greater than that associated with shrinkage and could have been sufficient to produce the dimensional change required by Viollet-le-Duc's theory. However, it is characteristic of creep phenomena that the greater part of the total deformation occurs soon after the loadings are applied. Recent tests on brick and lime mortar piers under constant load indicated that the creep deformation had for all practical purposes nearly ceased within fifty to one hundred days from application of the load.[15] A period of two to three months after the centering was removed from the vaults would have been the time during which the structure was in greatest danger from the effects of creep deformation. The collapse at Beauvais did not come until twelve years after completion of the vaults, which indicates that the failure was not directly due to this sort of movement.

A further argument against Viollet-le-Duc's hypothesis is that the colonnettes are clearly so slender in relation to their height that it is unlikely that an experienced medieval builder would have planned to use them to support any great weight. Of course, the fact that the vaults fell at Beauvais indicates that their builder did not possess infallible judgment in construction; yet the general success of medieval builders with long monolithic shafts, such as bar tracery of windows, shows that they must have been in the habit of waiting until the mass of coursed construction had settled before fitting monolithic shafts. Even if the upper construction at Beauvais had been hasty, the twin colonnettes would not have been placed until the mortar's shrinkage from drying had almost certainly ceased and the principal part of the creep deformation had quite probably occurred. And, as indicated earlier, additional long-term change from carbonation-shrinkage of the mortar would have been too insignificant to overload the colonnettes.

ANALYSIS OF THE CHOIR STRUCTURE

In the absence of a convincing hypothesis as to why the choir vaults of Beauvais fell, I initiated a photoelastic analysis in order better to understand their structure and, possibly, to arrive at a more conclusive explanation for the collapse. The analysis, though, had to be speculative, first, because the full nature of the original structure is unknown. Assumptions had to be made about such dimensions as the thickness of the original quadripartite vaults, the height of the rubble and mortar surcharges over the vault, and the cross section of some of the original members. Second, modeling usually takes a typical structural section for analysis, but in the Beauvais choir there is no typical bay. The lengths of the three bays of the original construction diminish from east to west, the proportions from east to west being approximately 25:42, 24:42, and 23:42. Because each bay is a different size, the loads also change from bay to bay. Inspection of the existing fabric shows that sections of the various pier buttresses and flyers in the hemicycle and choir also vary considerably.[16] Third, analyses of this type are usually facilitated by the as-

sumption that the whole structure can be adequately represented by a structural section; that is, that the resistance of the structure to dead weight and wind is largely in the plane of the section and that action outside the plane (in the third dimension) is negligible.[17] As discussed in chapter 2, the assumption of planar action is a reasonable one for nave or choir sections of High Gothic churches, but at Beauvais the choir is short, so there is likely to be some contribution to the support of the individual bays from the nearby more rigid structures of the hemicycle and transept. The varying lengths of the choir vaults indicate that the horizontal thrust components in the east-west direction from adjacent vaults will not balance each other, and this too contributes to action outside the north-south plane of a structural section. Even so, a three-dimensional model of the entire choir is not necessary as long as these limitations are kept in mind for the eventual interpretation of the model experiments.

The section that was drawn by Benouville (figure 36) was chosen for modeling because it is the only structural section of the choir that appears not to have been involved in the collapse and hence is most likely to resemble the original construction of the choir's other straight bays. The configuration of the high vaults was considered to be similar to that of Cologne (chapter 8); scaled colonnettes were incorporated in the model to test their behavior under expected loads.[18]

The results of the wind-load (plate 6) and dead-load experiments confirmed the reservations about many previous theories concerning the collapse of the vaults. They show that structural problems were not likely to be present in either the piers or the colonnettes. The highest compression stress level in the original choir piers under combined dead and wind loads was 28 kg/cm² (400 psi) at their bases; and the maximum compression in the clerestory wall was 21 kg/cm² (300 psi) under combined loads. As already observed, these values are typical for High Gothic construction. Likewise, the colonnettes under dead and wind loads bore at most 7,000 kg (15,000 lbs) each, significantly less than the axial load required to buckle them. The analytical results of the experiments, therefore, discount theories of the failure that depend upon the slenderness of either the piers or the colonnettes.

However, the analysis produced a further result that suggested a new hypothesis. The dead-load experiment revealed that just above the side aisles and just below the junction with the lower flyers, the intermediate pier buttresses were bent by horizontal forces large enough to initiate cracking (see section C-D and region R in figure 38). When the tensile stresses on the exterior portion of the leeward intermediate pier buttress caused by wind loading were added to those already present from the dead loading, the indicated total tensile stress was 18 kg/cm² (260 psi) on the inside edge above the aisle and 15 kg/cm² (210 psi) on the outside edge below the flyers. On the windward intermediate pier buttress, the wind load combined with the dead load yielded tensile stresses of approximately 5 kg/cm² (70 psi) on the inside edge below the flyers. Cracking would have occurred in the mortar well below these levels of stress. Moreover, since the tensile stress on the buttresses would have alternated as the wind changed direction, cracks could have developed on both sides, and these cracks are so located that they probably would have avoided detection. The upper critical regions, near the flyers, would not have been readily accessible, and the lower cracks would have been concealed by a gabled, side aisle roof.

Though the experimental results were derived from an estimated "worst wind," winds of lower velocities could still have produced the predicted cracking. Since wind forces vary as the square of the wind velocity, two-thirds of the velocity of the worst wind would produce roughly one-half of the load simulated in the test. The resulting tensile stresses still exceeded the capacity of medieval masonry construction. Less violent storms that might have occurred relatively frequently, therefore, could have cracked the intermediate pier buttresses. Perhaps, even within the period of twelve years, cracking under alternating wind loads could have caused an intermediate pier buttress to deteriorate so badly that the horizontal forces acting on it might have caused a section to slide from its support. If an intermediate pier buttress had collapsed, the system of flying buttresses above it would have been unsupported at its center, causing the flyers to fall, allowing the horizontal thrust of the high vaults to push out a section of the clerestory wall and trigger the sequential fall of additional vaults.

There is some irony in the fact that the critical portion of the intermediate pier buttress most subject to cracking is cited by Viollet-le-Duc as an example of rational design.[19] Since the upper portion of the intermediate pier buttress is off center and only balanced on its lower support (figure 38), Viollet-le-Duc argued that it would tend to incline towards the clerestory to help to resist the thrust of the high vault. To illustrate his argument he drew an analogy with a system of inclined props (figure 44). Actually the buttress does not lean inward under its dead weight because, as Viollet-le-Duc himself stated, its center of gravity is still over the support. Further, for the buttress to act as he suggested, it must implicitly be assumed that hinges exist just above the side aisle and at the points of attachment to the flying buttresses. Since hinging in masonry construction is tantamount to its cracking, this explanation of the overhanging action might actually be taken as a demonstration of the structure's problems rather than its rationality.

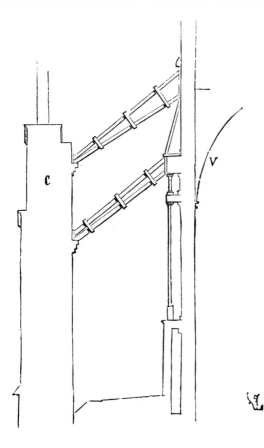

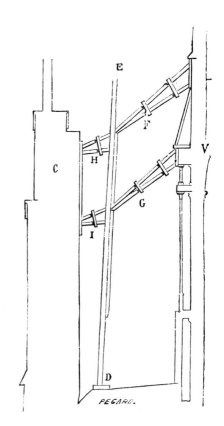

44 Intermediate pier
buttress as a prop. Sketch
by Viollet-le-Duc.

Viollet-le-Duc's failure to understand the behavior of the pier buttresses is not surprising because the structural behavior of Beauvais is not intuitively obvious. He correctly sensed, however, that the relatively stiff exterior pier buttresses do not receive as much horizontal force from the vaults and wind as might be expected. In fact it is the extra share of these loadings that was received by the far more slender intermediate pier buttresses that caused them to bend and might have led to their deterioration.

THE RECONSTRUCTION

The experiments described here have not settled the question about whether the colonnettes were used as Viollet-le-Duc imagined, but they do show that even if they had been part of the original construction, they need not have played any role in the collapse of the vaults. Failure of one of the intermediate pier buttresses could have brought down all of the choir vaults, leaving, because of its greater stability, only the hemicycle.[20] If failure of an intermediate buttress was indeed the cause of collapse and the fact was known to the rebuilders, some aspects of the reconstruction and the existing fabric can more readily be explained.

It is likely that in the aftermath of the collapse the overhang of the intermediate buttress was noticed. If the rebuilders then understood that this buttress absorbed some of the transmitted thrust from the flying buttresses and that it was the locus of the failure that had caused the collapse, they would have tried to take steps to prevent a repetition. Such steps would have included measures to ensure that the horizontal shearing loads transmitted into the intermediate buttress were reduced, that the buttress support was made more stable, and that the buttress itself was increased in strength and was better supported laterally.

Examination of the existing fabric shows that all these steps were, in fact, taken. Replacement of the quadripartite by sexpartite vaults can be interpreted as an attempt to reduce the horizontal loads because the extra pier extensions needed to support the new vault would have absorbed some of the wind loads on the clerestory and hence reduced those transmitted to the intermediate pier buttresses through the flyers.

Moreover, the four western intermediate pier buttresses, two on the north and two on the south of the choir, that were rebuilt after the collapse, are of far greater section than those in the last straight bay and those in the hemicycle (the two types are illustrated in figure 45). Part of this increase is explained by their role in receiving the transept flyers (where those flyers are in place), but the buttresses are also much deeper in the north-south direction, that is, in the direction of the horizontal vault thrusts and wind loads, which they are therefore better able to carry than their predecessors. In addition, the intermediate pier buttresses are not only stronger but their centers of gravity also appear to have been moved outward from the overhanging position.[21]

At the easternmost straight bay on the north side, an intermediate pier buttress that is largely original has been reinforced substantially at its base in the region that we have indicated as being subject to severe cracking (figure 43). There is also a third and lowest set of flyers abutting this and other intermediate pier buttresses at mismatched elevations, and on those intermediate pier buttresses without the additional flyers, there are iron bars or traces of them in similar positions (figure 33). Benouville offered the suggestion that the lowest flyers had been added in the sixteenth century to prevent the separation of the solid masonry addition from the pier extensions. His dating of the addition is suspect because some of these flyers are not filleted at their

45 Intermediate pier but-
tresses on the south side
of Beauvais Cathedral.
Note the greatly in-
creased section of the
rebuilt buttress
(foreground).

ends, as was sixteenth-century practice, and such flyers are used elsewhere at Beauvais. It is also implausible that if the flyers and iron bars were intended solely to hold the added masonry to the pier extensions, more than just an interior flyer or bar would have been constructed.

It is certainly more likely that the mismatched sets of flyers and bars were intended to support the intermediate pier buttresses, especially those around the hemicycle. In the hemicycle, where the vaults did not collapse, extensive rebuilding of the intermediate pier buttresses would have been uncalled for and difficult, since provision for support of the flyers and vaults would have had to be made during the work. In the choir proper, on the other hand, the intermediate buttresses could have been rebuilt completely and easily, whether one or all of them fell during the collapse, since reconstruction of the vaults would have followed the reconstruction of the buttress system. The alteration of the pier extensions all around the choir might have been considered necessary to receive the extra flyers and iron bars that were to be added to support the intermediate pier buttresses.

Although the mode of reconstruction of the choir appears to provide evidence to support this analysis, the new theory of the cause of the collapse of the high vaults in 1284 cannot be proved beyond a doubt because so much of the primary evidence disappeared so long ago. In 1975, however, when Stephen Murray, an architectural historian at Indiana University, examined the fabric of the cathedral with me, his archaeological observations further supported the basis of the model study on which this theory depends. In his view, the locus of the collapse was indeed the middle bay of the choir, which corroborated my assumption that this section must have been the weakest link, because the other bays were reinforced by the nearby rigid structures of the hemicycle and transept.[22]

This combination of archaeological observation and structural modeling can be immensely helpful in furthering our general understanding of how Gothic structures work. Particularly for Beauvais, the archaeological findings would seem to substantiate my hypothesis regarding a question of structural behavior that had baffled earlier investigators.

NOTES

Material for this chapter was derived from Maury I. Wolfe and Robert Mark, "The Collapse of the Vaults of Beauvais Cathedral in 1284," *Speculum* LI (July 1976):462–476. A recent, full account of the early history of Beauvais is given by Stephen Murray in "The Choir of the Church of St. Pierre, Cathedral of Beauvais: A Study of Gothic Architectural Planning and Constructional Chronology in its Historical Context" (see note 22).

1 Robert Branner, "Le Maître de la Cathédrale de Beauvais," *Art de France* II (Paris, 1962): 77–92.

2 Edward Corroyer's drawing in *L'Architecture Gothique* (New York: Macmillan, 1891) is actually a symmetric (right-left) inversion of the existing structure. The drawing shows the southern half-section as if it were viewed from the west; the small stairturret is, however, on the east face of the pier buttress.

3 Eugène E. Viollet-le-Duc, *Dictionnaire raisonné de l'architecture française du XIe au XVIe siècle*, 10 vols. (Paris: Librairies-Imprimeries Réunies, 1854–1868), IV, p. 175.

4 Paul Frankl, *Gothic Architecture* (Harmondsworth, England: Penguin Books, 1962), p. 101.

5 An example, particularly of differential settlement of towers, is found at Wells (chapter 6).

6 The higher quality of the masonry work of the first master compared to that of the builder of the upper fabric was pointed out by Léon Benouville, "Étude sur la Cathédrale de Beauvais," *Encyclopédie d'Architecture*, series 4, IV (1891–1892), pp. 52–54, 60–62, 68–70, and *tirage-à-part*.

7 A. P. M. Gilbert, *Notice historique et descriptive de l'église cathédrale de St. Pierre de Beauvais* (Beauvais, 1829), p. 10; Gustave Desgardins, *Histoire de la Cathédrale de Beauvais* (Beauvais, 1865), pp. 8ff., who cites as his source, Louvet, *Histoire et antiquitéz du diocèse de Beauvais* (Beauvais, 1635), 11, p. 474; L'Abbé L. Pihan, *Beauvais* (Beauvais, 1885), pp. 10ff.; Victor Leblond, *La Cathédrale de Beauvais*. Petites Monographies des Grands Édifices de la France (Paris: Henri Laurens, 1933), p. 15.

8 If the additional bracing of the attached shafts (see figure 35) is neglected, the pier core may be taken as a cylinder 14.6 m (48 ft) high and 1.5 m (4.9 ft) in diameter. Assuming an aggregate elastic modulus for the masonry of 200,000 kg/cm^2 (2,800,000 psi), the simple Euler equation (as described in any introductory text on strength of materials, for example, S. P. Timoshenko and D.H. Young, *Elements of Strength of Materials*, 5th ed. [Princeton: D. Van Nostrand, 1968]) yields a critical buckling stress that is two orders of magnitude greater than the nominal pier compression stress.

9 Jacques Heyman, "Beauvais Cathedral," *Transactions of the Newcomen Society* XL, 1967–1968 (London, 1971):20ff. Heyman's engineering analysis checks and elucidates Benouville's ("Étude sur la Cathédrale de Beauvais," plate 160) and confirms that the structure is stable under dead loadings. The method employed by both is a graphical-statical one which must assume the presence of "hinges" in a complex structure (see note 16, chapter 3). This method came into general use late in the nineteenth century and has been given new impetus by Heyman's work in limit analysis. See Jacques Heyman, "The Stone Skeleton," *International Journal of Solids and Structures* II (1966). The limit theorems extended by Heyman for use with masonry structures were developed originally and are used extensively for design of steel-framed structures. They provide a simple, reliable basis for determining safety factors against failure in structures of ductile materials, but they do not give information about their behavior under normal service loadings as do the elastic models described in this text.

10 Viollet-le-Duc, *Dictionnaire*, IV, pp. 180ff.; translation follows that of George M. Huss, *Rational Building* (New York: Macmillan, 1895), pp. 238ff. Heyman's account differs from Viollet-le-Duc's only on the specific nature of the movement of the block M (see Heyman, "Beauvais Cathedral," p. 30).

11 Viollet-le-Duc, *Dictionnaire*, IV, p. 179, fn. 1. Beauvais is one of the few major French High Gothic cathedrals that Viollet did not restore. Hence it may be assumed that he had no greater access than is available to present-day archaeologists.

12 Viollet-le-Duc's contention (*Dictionnaire*, IV, pp. 181ff.) that the use of monoliths, usually stones *en délit*, was a major principle and advance of Gothic construction is not consistent. *En délit* stones, like those of the colonnettes at Beauvais, are monoliths whose bedding plane is perpendicular to the natural sedimentary layering, or grain, of the rock from which it was cut. If a stone is bedded in this way and subjected to any substantial compressive stresses, it is likely to deteriorate more rapidly

than stone bedded with its grain because the compressive strain will cause tensile strains perpendicular to the beds and split or exfoliate the stones (Robert J. Schaffer, *The Weathering of Natural Building Stones*, reprint [Watford: Garston, 1972], pp. 14ff.). The *en délit* colonnettes could not resist tensile bending stresses unless securely tied to their sockets, top and bottom. Such ties would be difficult to construct, and if iron ties were used in any place subject to moisture, they would be a hazard to the stonework due to rust expansion (Schaffer, *Weathering*, pp. 22ff.). And, for the idea that the colonnettes consolidate the adjoining stonework, the most that can be said is that if this stonework is subjected to high loadings, the frictional forces among its constituents are likely to be more than sufficient to hold the masonry together.

13 Tests show the shrinkage of a lime mortar to be roughly 0.35 percent of its initial dimensions after eight days of drying, after which it remains essentially constant. See Sven Shalin, *Structural Masonry* (Englewood Cliffs, N.J.: Prentice-Hall, 1971), p. 200, fig. J. 10.

14 Carbonation of lime mortar is discussed in chapter 2. From tests of concrete blocks and structural members, it appears that carbonation shrinkage is from 0.03 to 0.1 percent of the member dimensions. See Frederick M. Lea, *The Chemistry of Cement and Concrete*, 3rd ed. (London: E. Arnold and Company, 1970), pp. 544–546; and Shalin, *Structural Masonry*, p. 200, fig. J. 9.

15 Creep tests on brick and lime mortar piers under constant load indicated that creep deformation for the whole masonry pier is of the order 0.1 to 0.2 percent of the pier height. See Shalin, *Structural Masonry*, pp. 202–208, fig. J. 12. b., fig. J. 16. a.

16 Heyman ("Beauvais Cathedral," p. 20) states that his analysis is for a typical bay. He is careful to note that at Beauvais only the structural section free of the transept and the hemicycle could be considered as typical; hence his sense of "typical" is different from that employed here. He misidentifies the section he means as typical as the one chosen by Benouville also. All of Benouville's drawings are of the structural section of the northern half of the easternmost straight bay. This can be confirmed by noting that the Benouville drawings contain a turreted stair tower on the pier buttress which, as drawn, could only be seen on the last straight section just at the hemicycle on the north ("Étude sur la Cathédrale de Beauvais," Plate 159, Plate 161).

17 In cases where this assumption is untenable, as in the study of the structural behavior of Gothic ribbed vaulting (chapter 8), a full three-dimensional model analysis must be undertaken.

18 The model was machined from a 7.1-mm (0.28-in) thick sheet of epoxy at a model-to-prototype scale of 1:144. After preliminary calculations and experimentation, a dead-load experiment and a wind-load experiment were designed. The dead loads were applied at a model-load scale of 1:127,000 to the vaults, flyers, and intermediate buttresses (see figure 15). The wind-load experiment assumed a mean peak wind of 155 km/hr (96 mph) at the roof peak height of 67 m (220 ft). The total loading on the section, taking the gust factor into account (see chapter 2), was calculated to be approximately 188,000 kg (415,000 lbs): 104,000 kg (230,000 lbs) on the windward side and 84,000 kg (185,000 lbs) on the leeward side. The wind load was modeled at a scale of 1:100,000. These wind loads are considerable even in relation to an estimated total fabric weight for one bay of 4,000,000 kg (8,800,000 lbs).

19 Viollet-le-Duc, *Dictionnaire*, IV, pp. 177ff., where it is discussed as the overhanging *culée* or the pier *porte-à-faux*.

20 Whether all the choir vaults fell cannot be settled here. If only one intermediate pier buttress were to fall, its collapse would almost certainly bring down the vaulting of one whole bay, likely more. Heyman, in "Beauvais Cathedral," p. 30, also maintains this point.

21 As evidenced in Benouville's drawing ("Étude sur la Cathédrale de Beauvais," Plate 161), the center of gravity of the heavier intermediate pier buttress is moved outward toward the exterior pier buttress.

22 Stephen Murray, "The Collapse of 1284 at Beauvais Cathedral," *The Thirteenth Century, Acta* III (1976):17–44. Murray also reported on a later problem of deformation of an intermediate pier buttress at Beauvais that necessitated rebuilding in 1517 and which further bears out the hypothesis of a design weakness in this important structural element. Although he did not then concur in the new theory developed in this chapter, Murray has accepted it in his most recent account of the vault collapse. See Stephen Murray, "The Choir of the Church of St. Pierre, Cathedral of Beauvais: A Study of Gothic Architectural Planning and Constructional Chronology in its Historical Context," *Art Bulletin* LXII (December 1980):533–551.

6

INNOVATION IN ENGLISH GOTHIC BUTTRESSING: THE REPAIRS TO THE TOWER OF WELLS CATHEDRAL

My interest in Wells Cathedral was initially engaged by modifications made to its structure in response to distress demonstrated by the fabric some time after its construction. But Wells (figure 46) is also a good example of the Early English Gothic style and, as such, serves as a contrast to the French High Gothic churches discussed in earlier chapters. Begun in the late 1180s, the construction of its nave and west front took place in the early decades of the thirteenth century while the campaigns of High Gothic construction in France were at their zenith. The style of Wells, however, differs markedly from its French contemporaries because the extremely high churches of France, which were later emulated in Germany, Italy, and Spain, were never adopted in England. Even Westminster Abbey, the tallest and most French of any English church in structure, has vaults which, at 31 m (102 ft), are significantly lower than its High Gothic contemporaries on the Continent. As the English architectural historian Peter Kidson has commented, the profile of Wells is, therefore, representative of the English type: "The tendency at Wells to stress the horizontal divisions of the building at the expense of the vertical was to become very characteristic of English Gothic in the thirteenth century; and it is one of the things which distinguishes English Gothic of this period from all Continental versions of the style."[1]

This tendency to horizontality in English churches contributed to another feature that distinguished them from continental churches. Although an earlier English architectural historian, Francis Bond, observed that "the practical, English [Gothic] builder avoided . . . mischief of rain, frost and storm" by eschewing exposed flying buttresses, it is the fact that, unlike their French counterparts, the English buildings were sufficiently low to maintain stability without them (figure 47).[2] Indeed, in many English churches, flying buttresses were only added later to prevent further spreading of clerestory walls or, often in the nineteenth century, to create a more romantic aspect.

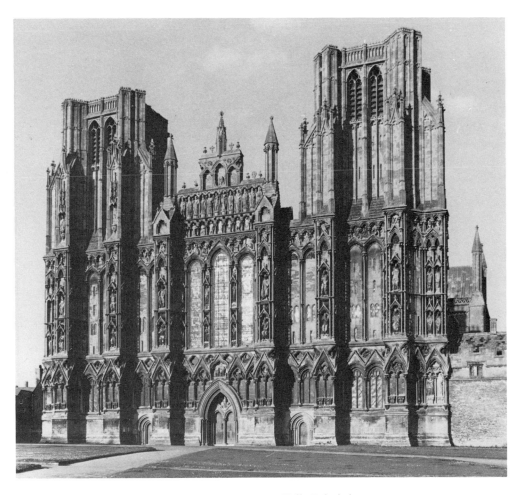

46 Wells Cathedral
from the west. Photo by
C. Malone.

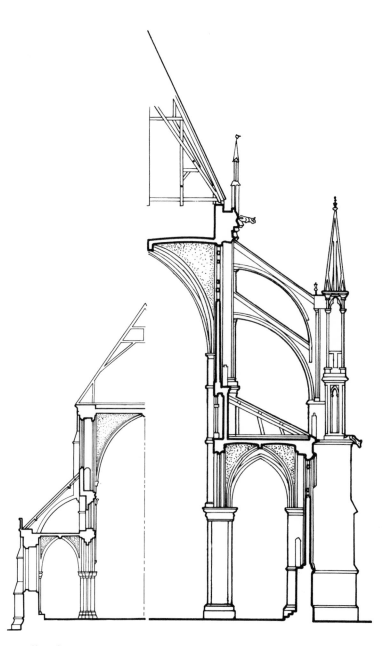

47 Wells and Reims
cathedrals. Comparative
nave cross sections in-
dicate the vast difference
in the *scale* of the structure of these two char-
acteristic buildings.

The differences in approach to Gothic design in France and England are often explained in terms of national style. For example, Kidson comments, "With a sure instinct, the English realized that their particular kind of Gothic was most effective when it was allowed to form long, receding vistas."[3] The English, already critical of so much that is French, have also criticized French High Gothic for at least the past three centuries on the ground of its extreme height and audacity of structure. Christopher Wren, for instance, in the seventeenth century, decried it as a *"Saracen* mode of building where nothing was thought magnificent that was not high beyond measure, with the flutter of arch buttresses. . . ."[4] It is, therefore, ironic that Westminster Abbey, where English kings have been crowned for centuries, was built largely according to a French design imported in 1245.[5] But this was an unusual success for the French, who, in a manner not unlike modern exporters of an industrial technique, had been more successful in disseminating their own style of Gothic elsewhere in Europe. Yet I am aware of no evidence to suggest that a comparable flow of technology crossed the Channel in the opposite direction.

Indeed, there is more to the difference between English and French Gothic design than style based on chauvinism. The French were, at the beginning of the thirteenth century, far ahead of the English from the technical point of view. The large scale and technical refinements of their buildings indicate the strength of the economic base necessary to produce them. The lower-profiled English buildings of the period were considerably less costly to produce and thus point to a less vital economic base. The fact that relative economic strength plays a part in creating regional differences in the architecture of large-scale buildings cannot be refuted, and it might, therefore, be observed that differences between the French and English Gothic structures of the thirteenth century owed as much to economics as to national proclivities.

48 Wells Cathedral.
The inverted arches were placed between the crossing piers after 1338.

CONFRACTE ET DEFORMATE

The original silhouette of Wells as it was completed in the middle of the thirteenth century, was uniformly long and low; even its towers were not prominent. Wells, however, suffered the fate of a number of churches when, around the beginning of the fourteenth century, it became the fashion to crown them with great towers and spires. These were better suited to the lower profiles of the English buildings than the gigantic constructions designed to scale with the higher Gothic churches on the Continent.[6] Nevertheless, because the English buildings, and particularly monastic establishments, were often sited near water on marshy soil, such additions frequently caused damaging settlement. This problem became apparent at Wells as a new tower and spire were raised over the central crossing piers after 1315.[7] The additional weight of the tower caused great distress to the earlier construction and necessitated measures to repair the damage. Part of this repair consisted of three sets of inverted arches placed between the piers of the crossing on the north, south, and west. Although the visual impact of these unique structures (figure 48) has made them a much discussed element of the building, some questions remain about their structural role.[8]

All histories of the cathedral written after 1870 that describe the inverted arches incorporate material from two lectures given at Wells in 1851 and 1863 by Robert Willis.[9] Willis was both a highly regarded architectural historian and, from 1837, Jacksonian Professor of Natural and Experimental Philosophy at Cambridge. His principal scientific work was in kinematics, the study of the motion of mechanisms (the anglicized, standard term for this branch of mechanics is his).[10] Statics of structures was not Willis's specialty, but he must have been familiar with the methodology of the subject, as he was in charge of the first documented, dynamic structural testing of beams for railway bridges along with the development

of mathematical theory for their deflection under dynamic loading.[11] Given these qualifications, Willis's view of the reworking of the structure of Wells has been held to be definitive.

From records preserved at Wells, Willis traced early diocesan convocations that authorized various campaigns of construction and repair. According to the summary of his lectures, "the convocation [of 1338] was summoned because the church was so enormously fractured and deformed ('enormiter confracta . . . totaliter confracte et deformate') that its structure [could] only be repaired, and with sufficient promptitude by the common counsel and assistance of its members." As a result of the convocation's actions, in Willis's words, "the great piers of the tower were [en]cased and connected by a stone framework which was placed under the north, south and west tower-arches, but not under the east." Willis also noted that "the original, high narrow windows had been fortified with later insertions, by way of bonding and stiffening the structure endangered by the sinking of its piers below, and producing on the outside a singular mosaic of styles in which later canopy and panel work is inserted in the earlier openings."

Willis's experience and the respect with which he is regarded have led to the assumption that he applied his technical expertise to his analysis of the function of the repairs at Wells.[12] The lectures, however, gave no indication that he in fact made use of any structural theory to verify his premise that the inverted arches acted to stabilize the tower piers.[13] Once this doubt is cast on Willis's analysis, the function of the inverted arches is open to further query. I decided to reexamine Willis's theory by means of a relatively straightforward analysis that requires no physical model. It is, instead, based on observations of settlement in the piers and alterations of the building fabric, an estimate of the weight of the fourteenth-century tower and its supporting structure, and a simple evaluation of the structural capacity of the structural elements that reinforce the tower.

ANALYSIS

The most important observation in the first instance was that the settlement is largely a problem of the western crossing piers only, with the most extreme settlement occurring in the northwest pier. This was apparent because string courses above the arcading in the nave and the western walls of the transept deform downward near the crossing piers; the crossing tower, along with the nave piers, leans westward; and buttressing has been added to the nave and western transept walls, partially blocking off clerestory windows and triforium openings in bays adjacent to the tower. Furthermore, if the inverted arches were indeed intended to tie together offending piers, the location of the three arches (on the north, south, and west sides of the crossing), and the absence of a fourth to the east, points also to a problem in the western piers. Having located the problem in the settlement of these two piers, I then turned my attention to the structural performance of the wall buttresses and inverted arches that were added after 1338 in an effort to prevent any further settlement.

Unlike the inverted arches, which are the most striking feature of the church's interior, the wall buttresses are unobtrusive (figures 49 and 50). Their construction, particularly their coursing, indicates that they were conceived to function in the manner of very steeply sloped flying buttresses, carrying mainly vertical loading from the tower to the piers adjacent to it. As with any flying buttress, they also contain horizontal components of force that must be met at each end of the buttress by adequate support.

At the top of the buttresses, this support is supplied by the crossing arches just below the vaults, and at their base by the gallery floors and walls. Thus although the buttresses are relatively slight, their form, which places the constituent stones primarily in compression, is most efficient for masonry, and they are likely to serve well in helping to support the tower.

On the other hand, further investigation suggests that the inverted arches are not as successful as the wall buttresses in their structural task. Although the arches have been described as "strange flying buttresses" because of their appearance, they do not act like flying buttresses in the structural sense. Flying buttresses act through efficient compression of their constituent stones. The inverted arches, however, act as a monolithic truss because they are tied together by stone rings within their spandrels. The rigid action of this truss in transmitting the pier loading across the spans of the arches, rather than in compression, results in shearing action under which stones tend to slide vertically, with concomitant tensile cracking. (The supporting action of the arches and buttresses is depicted in figure 51.)

A comparison of the effectiveness of the inverted arch system and the wall buttresses may be derived from an estimate of their relative strength. The minimum cross-sectional area of the two wall buttresses supporting each western pier is about 0.4 m² (4 sq ft), and the cross-sectional area at the center of the inverted arches (figure 52) is 1.7 m² (18 sq ft). The masonry may be assumed to easily accept 70 kg/cm² (1,000 psi) in compression without distress and an average shear stress across a section of 3.5 kg/cm² (50 psi), or equivalently 3.5 kg/cm² in tension, which is a generous estimate. Assuming stable supports, the maximum load that can be carried by each structural element is found by multiplying these stresses by the corresponding cross-sectional area.

The resulting maximum shear that the inverted arches can safely resist is then 59,000 kg (130,000 lbs), and the maximum vertical compression safely borne by the

49 Wells Cathedral.
Wall buttress in the nave.
Photo by M. Dean.

50 Wells Cathedral.
Wall buttresses in the
angle of the wall below
the crossing tower.

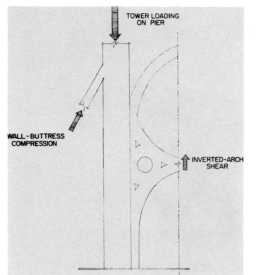

51 Wells Cathedral. Simplified mechanical diagram of inverted arch and wall buttress forces acting on a western pier.

wall buttresses is 245,000 kg (540,000 lbs). Thus the wall buttresses are more than four times as effective as the arches in supporting the pier.

These forces may be compared with an estimate of 2.3 million kg (5 million lbs) for the total dead-weight loading of the tower, the fourteenth-century spire, and the crossing piers (exclusive of the footings) made from observations of the existing structure and from drawings by one of the building's surveyors.[14] If a quarter of this total acts on each crossing pier, the wall buttresses could carry almost half of the pier loading. The inverted arches, however, could relieve the western piers of only about 10 percent of their load. Moreover, if they played even this minimum role, some evidence of tensile cracking would probably be evident at their center. There was, however, no sign of such distress when I examined the arches in 1974. Hence it may be concluded that the inverted arches carry even less than 10 percent of the tower loading.

This failure of the inverted arches to provide significant relief to the piers leads to speculation about their other possible functions. The only other role they could have had was to brace the piers laterally below the arches of the crossing in a manner similar to that achieved at Salisbury Cathedral with comparable but lighter inverted arches. However, the relatively low height of Wells, in which the springing of the crossing arches begins at only about 15 m (50 ft) above the floor, should have precluded the need for this additional lateral bracing.

In any event, it is possible that the reinforcement to the piers came too late, in the sense that the major damage arising from settlement had already taken place. Any discussion of the success of the reinforcement must take into account a typical characteristic of soils. With stable subsoil conditions (which is usually the case when the level of the water table remains constant), the rate of settlement in the foundations is greatest immediately after

52 Wells Cathedral. Section drawing showing disposition of wall buttress and inverted arch, by W. Shellman. The darkened section at gallery level is that of the inverted arches at the center of the nave.

53 Gloucester Cathedral.
The flying buttress
transfers some of the
weight of the crossing
tower.

new construction. It then decreases, often becoming imperceptible after about 10 to 20 years. In consequence, it may well have been that almost all the possible damage to the building from uneven settlement had already occurred by 1338 and that the reinforcement actually had little effect at that time. However, it could have helped to prevent further settlement during later alterations that added still more weight to the central tower.

It would appear, then, that any major role in stabilizing the piers of the crossing was played by the steeply sloped buttresses placed within the walls and not by the inverted arches, as Willis had assumed. The analysis used to arrive at this conclusion was within the scope of engineers of Willis's time, although estimates of masonry strength would not have been readily available. Willis, however, does not seem to have seriously considered the building in terms of the mechanics of its structure, even though the question posed was so overwhelmingly structural.

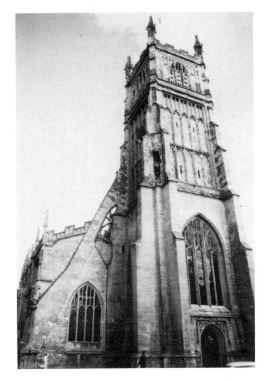

54 Cirencester parish church. The giant flying buttress helps to support the weight of the western tower.

The effectiveness of very steeply sloped buttresses of the type used at Wells was not, however, lost on the English masons of the fourteenth and fifteenth centuries who had to cope with placing towers over similarly poor foundations. Indeed, the use of flying buttresses to transmit *vertical* loadings to adjacent structure seems to have been an English, Late Gothic innovation. It is a variation on their use in French High Gothic churches, in which the flying buttresses were originally intended to provide mainly lateral support. For example, flying buttresses are found relieving the crossing piers of tower loadings at the English cathedrals of Salisbury and Gloucester (figure 53). At the parish church of Cirencester, a giant, almost vertical flying buttress carries a portion of the weight of the central western tower over to a footing at the outer perimeter of the building (figure 54).[15]

Even though the French fascination with tall structure and its subsequent refinement is missing from the original design of Wells, modifications made to the building over the years presented opportunities to test new structural ideas. As the present state of the building fabric attests, a scientific theory of structure was not necessary to achieve success; yet this analysis of the inverted arches illuminates the pitfalls of employing novel technical designs and, for that matter, historical analysis without recourse to analytical techniques.

NOTES

Material for this chapter was derived from: Robert Mark, "Robert Willis, Viollet-le-Duc, and the Structural Approach to Gothic Architecture" (see note 13). For Wells Cathedral, see Richard Morris, *Cathedrals and Abbeys of England and Wales* (New York: Norton, 1979).

1 Peter Kidson, Peter Murray, and Paul Thompson, *A History of English Architecture* (Harmondsworth, England: Penguin Books, 1965), p. 77.

2 Francis Bond, *Gothic Architecture in England* (London: Batsford, 1905), p. 371. Actually flying buttresses had been brought over to England at Canterbury in the 1180s, and the influence of that building brought about their emergence in a more developed form at Lincoln at the beginning of the thirteenth century. After the construction of Westminster Abbey, they were adopted by many English churches.

3 Kidson, Murray, and Thompson, *A History of English Architecture*, p. 77.

4 Christopher Wren, *Parentalia* (Farnborough, England: Gregg Press Limited, 1965; originally published in 1750), p. 298. It is particularly ironic that Wren specified flying buttresses to support the clerestory of St. Paul's Cathedral that are hidden from view by the massive screen walls along the perimeter of the building. See Harold Dorn and Robert Mark, "The Architecture of Christopher Wren," *Scientific American* 245 (July 1981):160–173.

5 Robert Branner, *Gothic Architecture* (New York: Braziller, 1961), p. 34.

6 For example, the crossing tower involved in the second disastrous collapse at Beauvais described in chapter 5.

7 Jean Bony, *The English Decorated Style* (Ithaca, N.Y.: Cornell University Press, 1979), p. 84.

8 Edward A. Freeman, *The History of the Cathedral Church of Wells* (London: Macmillan, 1870), pp. 118ff. Freeman, from his mid-nineteenth-century vantage point, considered that the inverted arches marred the appearance of the interior of the cathedral. He could accept what he termed their "clumsy ingenuity" only on the basis of constructive need.

9 Unfortunately, the lectures were never transcribed; there remains only a summary of the second lecture in the *Proceedings of the Somersetshire Archaeological and Natural History Society* XII (1863–1864):14–22.

10 Eugene S. Ferguson, "Kinematics of Mechanisms from the Time of Watt," *Bulletin of the U.S. Museum*, 228, Paper 27, Museum of History and Technology, Smithsonian Institution (Washington, D.C., 1962), pp. 209–213.

11 Published as an appendix to the account of the tests of the Conway and Britannia bridge sections by Fairbairn and Hodgkinson in the *Report of the Commissioners Appointed to Inquire into the Application of Iron to Railway Structures* (London, 1849). See also Stephen P. Timoshenko, *History of Strength of Materials* (New York: McGraw-Hill, 1953), pp. 173–178.

12 Sir Nikolaus Pevsner wrote that "Willis was much ahead of others in precision of description, clarity of thought and expansion of general theory . . . a standard of insight and meticulous accuracy which has never been surpassed." See *Some Architectural Writers of the Nineteenth Century* (Oxford: Clarendon Press, 1972), pp. 54ff.

13 Contrary to expectation, Willis does not appear to have taken a great interest in the structural rationale of English Gothic cathedrals. For example, in his *Architectural History of Canterbury Cathedral* (Oxford: Longman, Pickering and Bell, 1845), p. 228, he compared sections of the choir as it was before and after the fire of 1174. The post-fire section, largely the work of William of Sens until his near-fatal fall from construction scaffolding in 1179, embodies unusual, light flying buttresses slung low over the side aisle roof. If Willis is correct in showing their existence before the campaign of building was finished in 1185, then these flyers must be among the oldest now extant. The early flying buttresses employed in the nave of Notre Dame in Paris were dismantled in the thirteenth century, so their original disposition remains something of a mystery. The Canterbury choir, begun under the direction of a French master familiar with Notre Dame in Paris, could be a link to this very early flying buttress system. Willis, writing well over a century ago, might not have realized this, but it is puzzling that he made no comment about the use, or at least the appearance, of this important structural device at Canterbury. The absence of such comment is particularly noteworthy when one considers that for Willis's contemporary, Viollet-le-Duc, the flying buttress was the culminating example of the role of structural need redefining the whole aesthetic of medieval building. I found some explanation for Willis's reticence in reviewing his cultural milieu (see Robert Mark, "Robert Willis, Viollet-le-Duc, and the Structural Approach to Gothic Architecture," *Architectura* 7.2 [1977]:52–64). It should also be remembered that the form of the English Gothic cathedrals that concerned Willis was not as firmly tied to structural exigency as were the far higher, lighter French designs that occupied Viollet-le-Duc.

14 Charles Nicholson, "Construction and Design," *RIBA Journal* XIX (1912):627–628. See also John Britton, *The History and Antiquities of the Cathedral Church of Wells* (London: Longman, 1824), p. 98.

15 F. J. Allen, *Great Churches and Towers of England* (Cambridge: Cambridge University Press, 1932), p. 418. The fact that the giant flying buttress supporting the tower is also a distinguishing *visual* feature of Circencester provides a further example of structural need redefining the building aesthetic.

7

EXPERIMENTATION IN FOURTEENTH-CENTURY GOTHIC: THE CHURCH OF ST. OUEN, ROUEN, AND THE CATHEDRAL OF PALMA, MAJORCA

The year 1284, which marked the collapse of the high vaults of Beauvais, is frequently regarded as a turning point in the development of Gothic design. It is usually assumed that after that date the architects of large churches were more timid and hence less willing to carry out experiments in structure such as those that had produced the classic High Gothic buildings.[1] Yet the spirit of experimentation is still evident in the structural innovations introduced in two major buildings that were planned in the first half of the fourteenth century, one in Normandy and the other in the Balearic Islands, south of Barcelona.

ST. OUEN, ROUEN

Begun in 1318, the entire choir of the abbey-church of St. Ouen was standing in 1339, but it was not until almost the end of the Hundred Years War, in the second half of the fifteenth century, that the nave was completed. In spite of the long delay in construction, the building is quite unified, and the design, particularly of the interior elevation (figure 55), is generally regarded as a superb example of fourteenth-century Gothic.[2] The great windows in the clerestory and triforium show the influence of the French Rayonnant style, which developed in the Paris region in the mid-thirteenth century, and its giant scale (the keystones of its vaults are but five meters lower than those of Chartres) invites comparison of its structure with that of the classic High Gothic cathedrals.

As already observed, the lofty clerestory walls of the High Gothic churches are supported by a double tier of flying buttresses (and, at Chartres, by an additional tier as well). The lower tier is usually positioned to resist the outward, lateral thrust of the high vaults above the main arcades, while the upper tier resists the effects of wind forces on the upper clerestory walls and the high timber roof. The logic of this buttressing pattern is supported by the demonstration in chapter 2 that the

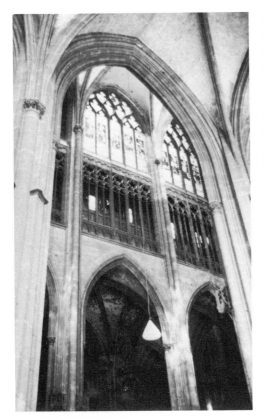

55 St. Ouen, Rouen. In the nave of this late Gothic church, the triforium is dissolved into a fine screen in front of large windows (which are blocked in this photograph).

forces generated by high winds on the superstructure of these large buildings are quite significant and can approach the order of magnitude of the horizontal thrusts of the high vaults.

St. Ouen, however, has only a single tier of flying buttresses. This tier was placed at an intermediate height, between the normal positions of the upper and lower tiers, and was apparently designed to resist both the vault thrust and wind loadings (figure 56). This was a daring step for so large a building, and its overall success has been proved by the survival of the church over the centuries. The unusual configuration, however, led me to investigate its effectiveness. Only after applying model analysis to the nave of the church did I realize that the design of the buttressing system was not, in fact, a complete triumph.

The nave structural system was modeled from a section drawn by A. C. Pugin early in the nineteenth century.[3] Under the scaled dead-weight loading, the model produced a photoelastic interference pattern that revealed a small amount of tensile stress in the pier extension just above the side aisle roof (figure 57). The level of this strss, 1.4 kg/cm² (20 psi), is below the threshold of tensile cracking, but the test served to reveal a possible region of weakness within the structure.

To arrive at wind loads, wind data for Rouen were obtained from twentieth-century meteorological records kept by the French government. The data indicated a maximum wind speed of 130 km/hr (81 mph) at the 43-meter (141-ft) elevation of the roof peak. The wind-load test results indicated bending in the leeward pier extension that caused tensile stress additional to that already present from the dead-weight loading. The total tensile stress from both dead weight and extreme high wind was 8.5 kg/cm² (120 psi) or about four times the estimated tensile strength of medieval mortar. Hence I was not surprised to find, when I visited St. Ouen shortly after completing the analysis,

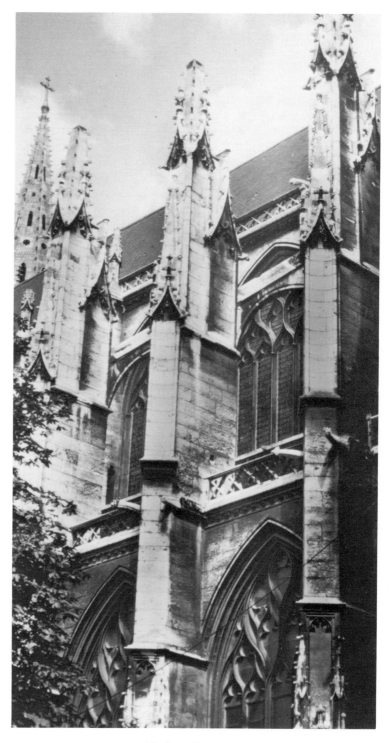

56 St. Ouen, Rouen.
The single, light flying
buttresses of the nave
were unique for a build-
ing of this scale.

evidence of a systematic pattern of crack-ing caused by tension in all of the pier extensions above the side aisles (figure 58, taken the year of my visit, 1969). Such cracks have obviously not been fatal to the building's structure, but they do require attention and repair so that weathering will not induce further deterioration.

Despite this slight structural malfunc-tion, St. Ouen succeeds in demonstrating an extreme of lightness and openness in the classic Gothic mode. While not as refined as St. Ouen in all of its construc-tion, Palma's structural innovation is even more radical.

THE CATHEDRAL OF PALMA, MAJORCA

The cathedral of Palma, Majorca, is one of the tallest Gothic churches in Europe (plate 9). When the design of the nave was conceived in the mid-fourteenth century, only the vaults of the choirs of Beauvais and Cologne exceeded its height. But be-cause of its remote site, relatively little has been written about this major building, and there is almost nothing in English.[4]

Construction of the cathedral began in the mid-thirteenth century, soon after the Christian reconquest of the Balearic Islands. A choir of modest size was largely completed in 1327, when all work on the cathedral seems to have been halted. A second campaign of construction, which raised the nave to its extreme height, was not begun until about 1357. The nave was erected one bay at a time, with the first prototypical bay completed in the 1370s. By the turn of the century, three bays were standing, but construction slowed afterward, and the nave was not completed until the sixteenth century.[5]

A comparison of the cross sections of Palma and Reims cathedrals (figure 59) serves to mark the structural evolution of Palma from the classic, High Gothic model. Although the very high arcading and unusually open side aisles of Palma evoke Bourges, its structure is

57 St. Ouen, Rouen. Photoelastic interference pattern in model under simulated dead-weight loading. The region above the side aisles, indicated by interference order (N) equal to 1.1, is ex-periencing tension.

58 St. Ouen, Rouen. Cracking distress in pier extension above the side aisles. (The triforium glass has been removed in this photograph.) Photo by F. Boucher.

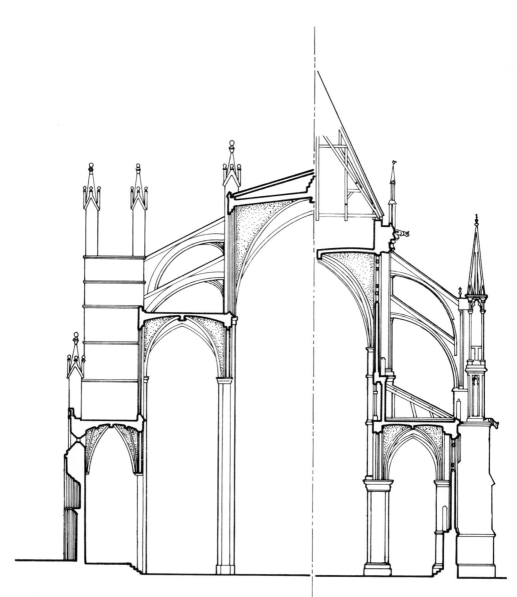

PALMA

REIMS

59 Palma and Reims
cathedrals. Comparative
cross sections through
the naves indicate the
enormous size and spa-
ciousness of the Palma
design.

unlike that of any other major High Gothic church. All its dimensions are gargantuan by comparison. The height of the vault keystone is 44 m (144 ft); the main arcade is 19.5 m (64 ft) wide; and the bays are 8.8 m (29 ft) long. Reims, in comparison, has a keystone height of 38 m (124 ft); arcade width of 14.5 m (48 ft); and bay length of 7.2 m (24 ft).

It is remarkable that despite these great spans, the hexagonal main piers of the arcade that support the high clerestory walls are extremely slender (figure 60). It is this particular aspect of Palma's design that sets it apart from its High Gothic antecedents and that contributes so powerfully to creating an atmosphere of vast spaciousness not unlike that of large halls built from modern materials.

The boldness of Palma's architect can be quantified. Table 1 compares Palma's pier dimensions and the pier slenderness ratio (calculated by dividing the pier's height by its width) with those of the major thirteenth-century High Gothic cathedrals. The slenderness ratio of the Palma piers is almost 50 percent greater than that of any earlier large church, and the visual and technical difference between Palma and the others is even more dramatic than the numbers suggest.[6] This difference arises partly because the piers at Palma are not surrounded by attached shafts like the piers of the earlier buildings. These shafts, which were not accounted for in table 1, in fact make the earlier piers heavier visually and also add considerable reinforcement to them, thereby making the achievement at Palma all the more extraordinary.

The gain in interior space at Palma was won by transferring the bulk of the building's structure to the exterior in the form of massive pier buttresses. These great buttresses, however, do not have a purely structural role. They also form the side walls of chapels set between them along the perimeter of the church. On the building's exterior, these chapels are marked by pairs of low buttresses standing

60 Palma, Majorca. The slender, coursed nave piers appear to be better suited to modern reinforced concrete construction.

61 Palma, Majorca. The flying buttresses of the nave here require shoring and additional wall arches to sustain them.

between the high pier buttresses. The visual rhythm set up by the modulation of the buttresses contributes to Palma's unique form.[7]

The size of Palma would alone have been sufficient reason for its study, but the combination of great size with singularly slender piers raised substantial questions about the functioning of the structure and made it a prime candidate for modeling.

The model section was derived from my own measurements and from drawings of the nave of the cathedral made by students of architecture at the University of Barcelona early in the twentieth century.[8] Dead-weight load distributions in the actual building were those used for an earlier statical study performed by one of the surveyors of the cathedral.[9] In the resulting photoelastic interference pattern (plate 10), the almost uniform color visible in the main piers under dead-weight loading indicates that the amount of bending present is so negligible as to be unique among the Gothic churches discussed in this text.[10] The results go far to explain the stability of these very slender, main structural elements.

The model was loaded a second time to determine the effect of wind loads. Data on wind velocity at Palma over the period 1943 to 1974 were obtained from the Ministerio del Aire and the Servicio Meteorologico Nacional in Spain and the Climatic Center of the United States Air Force. These data showed that the greatest mean wind velocity to be expected at the level of the cathedral roof was 130 km/hr (80 mph). When the resulting wind loads were applied to the model, the maximum stress throughout the structure proved to be low compared to the stress found in northern High Gothic churches. In the pier itself, it was only about 5 kg/cm² (70 psi). Even the combined maximum compressive stress in the pier from both wind and dead-weight loading—

27 kg/cm² (380 psi)—is about 20 percent less than the equivalent value for Amiens.

The only regions indicating possible structural problems were at the ends of the flying buttresses. Here, bending from the effect of winds added to the bending already present from the dead-weight loading produced tension of sufficient magnitude to engender cracking. In fact, several of the upper flying buttresses are propped by infill walls or columns between the tiers, which in turn require extra wall arches to reinforce the lower flyers (figure 61). These findings may shed some light on why some of the high vaults had to be rebuilt at the beginning of the eighteenth century—a repair mentioned by Marcel Durliat but with no hint as to the cause of their weakening.[11]

The form of the flying buttresses is mainly responsible for their difficulties. They are long and, more crucial, they are not sloped appreciably and are therefore subject to detrimental bending. Moreover, Palma has no high, pitched roof. Without it, the upper flyers, whose normal function in High Gothic buildings is to brace the structure against the wind loads on such a roof, serve little purpose, and the absence of loading only contributes to their malfunction. The builders of Palma might have supported the vaults more effectively if they had replaced the two tiers of flying buttresses with a single, more steeply sloped tier of the type used at Bourges and had placed transverse walls over the side aisles as at Laon.

Even though both the church of St. Ouen and the cathedral at Palma show some structural weaknesses, they achieved the objective of their designers through further evolution of Gothic structure. At St. Ouen, the classic Gothic wall and buttress system was further refined and lightened. At Palma, following in the southern tradition, the classic system was given even

Table 1 Gothic cathedral pier dimensions and slenderness ratios

Building site	Date[a]	Height[b] in m (ft)	Width[c] in m (ft)	Slenderness ratio
Chartres (nave)	1194	8.0 (26)	1.6 (5.2)	5.0
Bourges (choir)	1195	14.9 (49)	1.6 (5.2)	9.3
Reims (nave)	1211	9.6 (32)	1.6 (5.2)	6.0
Amiens (nave)	1220	12.5 (41)	1.5 (4.9)	8.3
Beauvais (choir)	1225	14.6 (48)	1.5 (4.9)	9.7
Cologne (choir)	1248	11.9 (39)	1.3 (4.3)	9.2
Palma (nave)	1357	22.0 (72)	1.6 (5.2)	13.8

a. Year construction was begun.

b. Distance from top of base to bottom of capital; that is, straight section length of load-bearing, coursed construction.

c. Diameter for round piers; distance between flats for hexagonal piers.

greater solidity on the exterior. This strategy permitted the piers to be reduced in size, which led in turn to the unique openness of the church's interior.

In general terms, however, the structural innovations of the fourteenth century did not go far beyond those of the thirteenth. In fact, until the industrial revolution brought with it the new building techniques of the nineteenth century, no period matched the development of building structure that took place, particularly in the Île de France, between the mid-twelfth and mid-thirteenth centuries, when the major technical problems of tall, skeletal stone construction were essentially solved by the introduction of such structural elements as the flying buttress. Although by the middle of the thirteenth century architects seem to have become more concerned with handling vast areas of glass and slender stone tracery than with achieving very tall buildings, this is not to say that all structural experimentation in tall Gothic buildings had ended. St. Ouen and Palma provide striking evidence that it had not.

NOTES

Material for this chapter was derived from Robert Mark, "The Church of St. Ouen, Rouen—A Re-examination of Gothic Structure," *American Scientist* 56 (Winter 1968):390–399; Robert Mark and Ronald S. Jonash, "Wind Loading on Gothic Structure," *Journal of the Society of Architectural Historians* XXIX (October 1970):222–230; and Robert Mark, "Structural Experimentation in Gothic Architecture," *American Scientist* 66 (Sept.–Oct., 1978):542–550. For further details on St. Ouen, see Whitney S. Stoddard, *Monastery and Cathedral in France* (see note 2). For Palma, Majorca, see Marcel Durliat, *L'Art dans le Royaume de Majorque* (see note 5).

1 See, for example, Louis Grodecki, *Gothic Architecture* (New York: H. N. Abrams, 1977), pp. 133ff.

2 Whitney S. Stoddard, *Monastery and Cathedral in France* (Middletown, Conn.: Wesleyan University Press, 1966), pp. 307ff. Julien Guadet selected St. Ouen, as we have seen, for a project in which he redesigned the structure using, in place of flying buttresses, more efficient parabolic arches derived from late nineteenth-century structural theory.

3 A. C. Pugin, *Specimens of Gothic Architecture* (London: Britton, 1823–1825). The model was made at a scale of 1:167. Dead-weight loads were applied at a scale of 1:325,000 and wind loads at a scale of 1:160,000.

4 There is a short monograph by the American Gothic revivalist architect, Ralph Adams Cram, *The Cathedral of Palma de Mallorca: An Architectural Study* (Cambridge, Mass.: The Medieval Academy of America, 1932). Palma's remoteness is suggested by the fact that the architect, George Edmund Street, who wrote what is probably the most comprehensive work in English on the Spanish Gothic, never saw it. This he regretted, writing that "so far as I can learn, it seems that the mainland owed much to Palma in the way of architectural development." See *Gothic Architecture in Spain*, 2 vols. (New York: B. Blum, 1969; originally published in 1865), II, p. 242. It is even more likely, though, that Palma owed much to developments at Barcelona, notably in the design of the Church of Santa Maria del Mar, begun in 1328.

5 The chronology is taken from Marcel Durliat, *L'Art dans le Royaume de Majorque* (Toulouse: ed. privat, 1962), pp. 150–167.

6 Cram wrote of Palma, "The vast and lofty nave is even more open and spacious than . . . any Gothic church in the North. It is a forest of silvery columns that open out into vaults without the interruption of conventional capitals, with, beyond, long ranges of vaulted chapels." See Ralph Adams Cram, *The Cathedral of Palma de Mallorca*, p. 7.

7 Heavy buttresses were used to flank chapels in the walls of fortified churches in southern France. Indeed, this element of Palma's design is likely to have been taken from French models such as the cathedral of Albi (begun in 1282).

8 I am indebted to Professor Juan Bassegoda of Barcelona University for making copies of these drawings available.

9 Juan Rubió-Bellver, "Conferencia acerca de los conceptos organicos, mecanicos y constructivos de la Catedral de Mallorca," *Anuario de la Asociacion de Arquitectos de Cataluna* (Barcelona, Spain, 1912):87–140. Rubió-Bellver worked with the Catalonian architect Antoni Gaudí on restoration of the cathedral at the beginning of this century. His work is the most comprehensive source of data on the building fabric. For the experiment, the structural section of the nave was modeled at a scale of 1:144. Dead-weight loadings were applied at a scale of 1:150,000 and wind loads at a scale of 1:21,650.

10 The indicated stress level in the piers corresponding to the model data is 15 kg/cm^2 (210 psi). But since the weight of the lower 30 m (98 ft) of the piers was not simulated in the test, the stress from the pier weight must be algebraically added to the stress from the model loading, giving a total compression stress at the base of the pier of 22 kg/cm^2 (310 psi), a moderate value for construction at such great scale.

11 Durliat, *L'Art dans le Royaume de Majorque*, p. 167.

8

GOTHIC RIBBED VAULTING: THE HIGH VAULTS OF THE CATHEDRALS OF COLOGNE AND BOURGES

As early as 1845, Robert Willis published a comprehensive article on the construction of medieval vaulting in which he observed that the Gothic ribbed vault "consists, as is well known, of a framework of ribs or stone arches, upon which the real vaults or actual coverings of the apartment [the vault web] rest. . . . The ribs are the principal features, and the surface of the vaults subordinate."[1] (Figure 62 is from Willis's article.) Willis's implication that the Gothic rib plays a predominant structural role in vaulting has since been widely accepted, perhaps because it was corroborated by Viollet-le-Duc, who regarded the rib as still another example of the rationality of the elements of Gothic structure.[2] However, Viollet-le-Duc's conviction, echoed by many other writers, was based more on the validity of visual impressions than on a comprehensive understanding of the structural action of vaulting.

Probably the most persuasive argument against the rationalist view of the structural function of the rib in vaulting is that of Pol Abraham. Before treating the much more complex structural action of vaulting, however, Abraham considered the simple arch within a single plane in space. Because the arch consists of voussoirs inclined at various angles with respect to the horizontal, Abraham contended that the major forces would also be carried at these inclined angles. A simple graphical operation resolves the oblique "resultant of the pressures," as Abraham calls it, into components—one horizontal and one vertical (figure 63).[3] At any given point in the arch, the magnitude of the vertical component is the sum of the weight of all the material between that point and the crown. If the oblique resultant acts at exactly the angle of inclination of the arch as Abraham assumed, there is a unique relationship between the three vectors of the triangle at that point, and it follows that the horizontal thrust is directly related to the weight of the vault.

62 Drawing by Robert
Willis of the early
sixteenth-century vaults
over the Henry VII
Chapel at Westminster
Abbey.

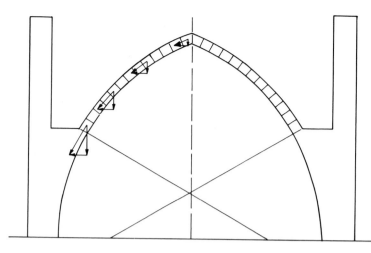

63 Force polygons for an
arch (after Abraham). In
this illustration, the lines
of action of the compres-
sive forces within the
arch correspond to the
arch centerline.

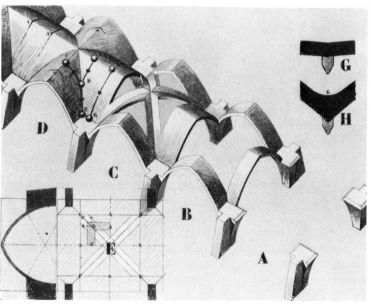

64 Vault behavior (from
Abraham). Abraham used
the rolling ball analogy
to trace the path of forces
within a vault.

While this line of reasoning gives a first approximation to the structural behavior of this relatively simple system, it overlooks the existence of bending, which can be crucial to the integrity of the arch. Specifically, the assumption that the resultant forces always follow the inclination of the arch violates the fundamental precept that all forces acting on a structure must be in equilibrium. Just as the vertical force components must balance the weight, so the horizontal force components acting at the two ends of any voussoir must offset each other; therefore, the horizontal force component in an arch loaded only by (vertical) weight must be *constant* throughout the span. The horizontal and vertical force components that satisfy this equilibrium do not necessarily combine to give a resultant force vector aligned with the inclination of the arch. When they do not, bending must occur because the resultant force tends to wander from the arch centerline, that is, the force becomes eccentric, as is demonstrated in the appendix (see "forces").

In short, the specific form of the arch in relation to how it is loaded has great influence in producing bending, an action not accounted for in Abraham's interpretation. This effect can become a particularly serious problem when the eccentricity becomes large enough to compress one side of a member while stretching the other. Even a structure with good compressive strength will suffer distress from any significant amount of bending if it does not also possess tensile capacity, and, as we have observed, masonry construction is notorious for its poor tensile strength. Hence, Abraham's arch analysis is overly simplistic, and when he attempted to extend it to explain the much more complex behavior of a three-dimensional vault, his difficulties multiplied.

Abraham considered the vault to be composed of arrays of parallel arches. This view led him to develop his famous analogy in which the direction of a marble rolled from the top ridge of the vault (see figure 64)—either in the "direction of the greatest curvature" (along the path of an "arch") directly to the pier or toward the groin and then down the groin towards the pier—indicated the direction taken by the forces within the vault.[4]

According to this analogy, therefore, the curvature of the webbing directs forces to the groin. At the groin, as Abraham inferred from cross sections of the vault, there is an *arêtier*, or natural rib, formed by the intersection of the vault webs. This thickened webbing (figure 64H), according to Abraham, was sufficient in itself to carry the forces and transmit them diagonally to the pier without resort to ribs.[5]

The marble analogy is but one of several arguments Abraham used to arrive at the conclusion that the basic statics and behavior are the same in a vault with ribs and a vault without ribs.[6] According to him, the ribs accept no loading from any part of the vault proper, and do not alter the direction of the forces within the vault. They are, therefore, useless in a structural sense.

The lively controversy in the literature of the history of architecture that largely resulted from these observations led Paul Frankl to review much of the commentary on vaulting and express despair that even physicists did not agree among themselves as to the role of the rib.[7] Yet despite all the arguments and the weightiness of the writing on this subject up to and after Frankl's review, no one has attempted to resolve the question by using quantitative structural analysis of a complete vault system. It was this realization that led to the attempt described here to determine the true role of the rib by analyzing some actual vault configurations using three-dimensional models.

THREE-DIMENSIONAL MODELING

The general configuration of quadripartite, ribbed vaulting shown in plate 7 was originally found in the high vaults of all the major High Gothic churches save Bourges.[8] The vaults of two bays in the choir of Cologne Cathedral were chosen for an initial study because more information was available on them than on the vaults of any other High Gothic church.[9]

A model of their configuration without ribs was constructed at 1/50 scale from components that were machined from an epoxy cylindrical casting (figure 65). Each vault segment was taken as part of a surface having a variable radius about a single axis as shown in figure 66, allowing the model to be assembled from four components. These represented right- and left-hand longitudinal and transverse webbings. Loadings were placed on the finished model, which was then put through a heating cycle as described in chapter 2.[10] After cooling, the model was observed in a polariscope to study the locked-in photoelastic patterns. Slices of sections were then taken from it to reveal internal stress distributions. The structural action of the model, including magnitudes, distributions, and directions of structural forces, as well as thrusts directed at the piers, was quantitatively determined from these data and used with scaling theory to predict the structural action of the full-scale vault system.[11]

Although three-dimensional photoelastic modeling is a very powerful analytic tool with remarkable ability to pinpoint critical regions requiring special care in design, it has the limitation that the model must be reconstructed following a first testing and slicing if variations in loading and geometry are to be studied. In this case, a totally new model would have to be reproduced. However, numerical computer modeling, which can feasibly handle a structural geometry as complex as groined vaulting, is now available. Although programming requires much time-consuming, patient effort, once it is done, the computer models can be used to study any number of load and geometric modifications without difficulty.

Numerical modeling involves the same procedure as that used with a physical model. The model's form, however, is described by a series of coordinates taken at intervals on the structure's surface. These coordinates define a mesh that becomes the geometric model for the computer. A series of equations related to loading conditions and the properties of the materials involved are then used to calculate the displacement at all the mesh points (almost 750 points for the model in this study) in order to obtain the displacement pattern for the entire structure. That pattern then gives, through equations of elasticity, the same type of information about the overall distribution of structural forces as the results of the photoelastic model test.

If the results from the numerical model demonstrate close agreement (within, say, 10 percent) with those from the physical model, the numerical model can be used with an even greater degree of confidence to study modifications to the original configuration. Agreement is all the more important in this case because our knowledge of vault geometries is incomplete. No detailed drawings exist for the vaults of any of the major medieval churches (although photogrammetric studies now in progress may soon remedy this situation). The only accurate information usually available is what one can ascertain with tape measure and plumb line, such as the distance from the floor to the crown of the vaults.

For the purposes of this study, therefore, it was important that the height of three points along the top of Cologne's choir vaults and the height of the top of its clerestory windows were known. This information permitted the upper surfaces of the vaults to be represented approximately by a mathematical expression giving the radius of vault curvature at any

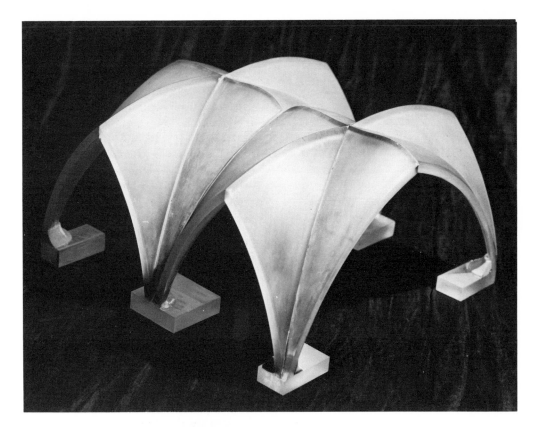

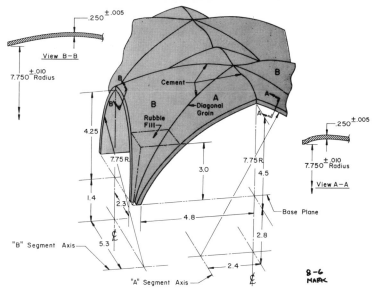

View B-B

.250 ±.005

7.750 ±.010 Radius

Cement

Diagonal Groin

Rubble Fill

B

A

B

B

A

A

4.25

7.75 R

3.0

1.4

2.3

4.8

5.3

2.4

"B" Segment Axis

"A" Segment Axis

7.75 R

4.5

2.8

Base Plane

.250 ±.005

7.750 ±.010 Radius

View A-A

8-6 MARK

65 Photoelastic model of Cologne vaulting is composed of individually machined epoxy sections joined by epoxy cement.

66 Cologne vault model geometry (dimensions in inches).

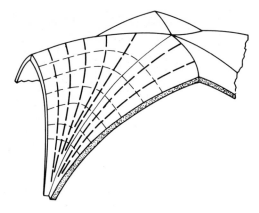

67 Vault force trajectories under dead-weight loading. Heavy dashed lines indicate the paths of maximum compression forces.

point. (Typical sections of these surfaces are shown as A-A and B-B in figure 66.) The geometries of both the photoelastic model and the initial computer model followed this approximate formulation.

Results from the unribbed numerical model of the choir vaults at Cologne agreed well with those from the unribbed photoelastic model. Hence the following summary of observations from the first series of tests can be derived from either modeling approach:

1. The only observed region of high compressive stress is where the vault joins the pier. It is possible that the ribs may have been employed here as a device to reduce local vault stresses, although the maximum highly localized stresses of 28 kg/cm² (400 psi) in the unribbed 33-cm (13-in) thick vaults do not exceed maximum values found in other regions of typical High Gothic churches.

2. Bending moments throughout the vault are low so that tensile stresses caused by the dead weight of the vault and rubble fill (figure 66) are almost nonexistent. While the rubble fill may perform a function in helping to transmit thrust more uniformly to the supporting buttressing system (and helping to support the pier extensions against inward-acting forces, as discussed in chapter 2), its weight has no significant effect on the overall performance of the vault.

3. The horizontal component of thrust of an (unribbed) Cologne high vault is 26,000 kg (57,000 lbs) as compared to a vertical force of 77,000 kg (170,000 lbs). These calculations are based on a total vertical vault loading of each full bay equal to 154,000 kg (340,000 lbs), including the rubble fill.

4. The major in-plane compressions are directed toward the pier extensions that support the vault, as shown by the heavy, dashed lines of figure 67. They do *not* follow the trajectory of a rolling marble, as suggested by Abraham. The significance

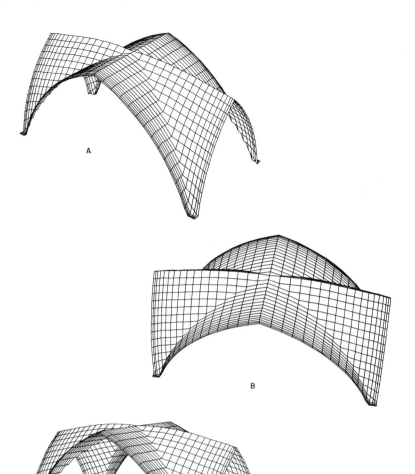

68 Three computer-drawn
perspective projections
of quadripartite vaulting.
The geometry of this
vault configuration is
very similar to that of the
Cologne vault model in
figure 66.

69 Vertical (V) and horizontal (H) forces (reactions) at the supports of quadripartite vaults.

of this important finding will be discussed at a later point.

It should be added that the general state of compression observed throughout the vault again validates the modeling assumption that the full-scale, articulated construction can be represented by a monolithic model.

QUADRIPARTITE RIBBED VAULTING

The formulation of the geometry used in the computer study of the unribbed vault is not easily adapted to other modifications. For this reason, an analytic form with a very similar geometry to figure 66 but with the potential to accommodate the necessary modifications was adopted. The computer was used to draw perspective projections and aid in reaching the final version of this form. Once the geometry was stored in the computer, it could be recalled as it would be seen by an observer from any vantage point (see views in figure 68).

Vertical and horizontal reactions (see figure 69) for the vault configuration illustrated in figure 68 were obtained from the computer model under four different conditions: without the ribs but with the fill (as in the photoelastic model tests); without the ribs or the rubble fill; with the ribs but without the fill; and with both the ribs and the fill. The results are listed as cases 1 through 4 in table 2 and are compared with those for the photoelastic model, which are reported as case 5.[12]

In cases 1 through 4 the stresses everywhere within the vaults, except in the region where the vault joined the pier, were low, of the order of 1 kg/cm² (14 psi) compression. Near the point where the vault joined the pier, the maximum local compressive stress in case 1 was 18 kg/cm² (255 psi). When the loading was shared by ribs, as in cases 3 and 4, this figure was reduced to 5 kg/cm² (70 psi).[13] Computer results for axial and bending stresses in the diagonal and transverse ribs indicated that in almost all sections the average compressive stress carried by the rib was far greater than any tensile stress resulting

Table 2 Vertical (V) and horizontal (H) reactions for vault configurations of figure 68
(cases 1 through 4) and photoelastic model of figure 66 (case 5)

Case	Ribs	Rubble fill	Forces × 1,000 kg (lbs) V	H	H/V
1	No	Yes	78 (172)	28 (62)	0.36
2	No	No	53 (117)	25 (55)	0.47
3	Yes	No	66 (145)	29 (63)	0.43
4	Yes	Yes	91 (200)	31 (69)	0.35
5	No	Yes	77 (170)	26 (57)	0.34

70 Vaulting in the choir
of the abbey church of
Saint-Étienne, Caen.
Analysis results show
that cracking in the
webbing caused by out-
ward displacement of the
wall has little effect on
overall vault behavior.

from bending alone. In the few sections where bending stress combined with the average axial compressive stress produced a small amount of tension in the ribs, the tension was only 0.2 or 0.3 kg/cm² (3 or 4 psi).

The directions of the major compressive forces were found to flow, as before, along the shortest paths through the shell toward the point of support at the pier (as depicted in figure 67). This typical compressive behavior indicates that cracks often seen in webbing along these flow lines are relatively unimportant to the overall performance of the vault and that some outward motion of the clerestory, such as that illustrated in figure 70, can be tolerated. And once again, as in the case of the study of the unribbed vault, the validity of using a monolithic model to represent the full-scale, articulated structure was confirmed.

A final modification of the Cologne geometry was made to test the structural effect of doubly-curved versus singly-curved webbing. The behavior of a computer-produced, singly-curved, quadripartite surface (figure 71), including both fill and ribs, indicates similarity to that of the doubly-curved prototype in all respects, particularly in the directions taken by the forces in the web. The forces at the supporting pier extensions for both doubly-curved and singly-curved vaults are also similar; the vertical reactions differ by a bit more than 2 percent, and the horizontal reactions differ by less than 1 percent.

Hence characteristic English vaulting, which approximates single curvature, appears to behave in much the same fashion as the typically French, doubly-curved vaulting. Furthermore, the fact that the behavior of the vault was not markedly different whether it was singly or doubly curved made simpler the task of studying the sexpartite vault. It suggested that one could determine the general structural characteristics of doubly-curved, sexpartite vaulting by using the model of a simpler, singly-curved vault.

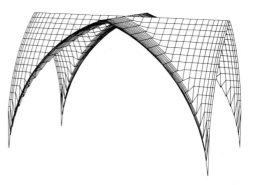

71 Computer-drawn, singly-curved, quadripartite vaulting.

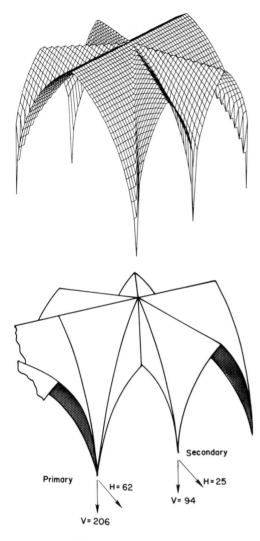

72 Computer-drawn
sexpartite vaulting.

73 Sexpartite vaulting.
Forces at the supports (in
thousands of pounds).

SEXPARTITE RIBBED VAULTING

The approach to generating the more
complicated sexpartite geometry was
essentially the same as that described for
the quadripartite geometry. However, there
was much less information available for
describing the shape of a typical sexpartite
surface (plate 8). Branner's drawing of
the Bourges choir section was chosen as
a starting point.[14] Portions of the vault
were assumed initially to be of constant
radius and, again, the vault surface was
formulated with the aid of computer-
drawn projections (figure 72).

Assumptions and simplifications were
the same as those used in the studies
of quadripartite vaulting and, because the
rib sizes and web thicknesses of Cologne
and Bourges were similar, the same
dimensions were used for both studies.[15]
This procedure both simplified the analysis
and also enhanced comparisons between
the quadripartite and sexpartite vaults
by minimizing other variables.

As in the quadripartite vaulting, the
principal compressive forces in the sexpartite vaults were found to flow through
the webs in the shortest path towards
the nearest pier. Hence, the ribs have
no more structural importance in sexpartite vaulting than they do in the less complicated quadripartite system. This is
further demonstrated by figure 73, which
shows that the ratio of forces at the primary and secondary piers in the sexpartite
vault is not directly related to the number of ribs joining each one, as might
be expected if the ribs, in fact, supported
a major portion of the load from the vault.
Indeed, it is the geometry and the loading pattern of the entire vault that determine the forces found at the piers rather
than the number of ribs that join each
pier.

Another significant comparison between the two systems of vaulting concerns the relationship of weight and

horizontal thrust. The bays of the vaults of Bourges and Cologne are of similar dimensions; that is, the transverse and longitudinal spacing of the piers in the two buildings is similar and the rise of the vaults is about the same. The total vault system weights including ribs and fill are 270,000 kg (600,000 lbs) for the Bourges (singly-curved) sexpartite vault and 370,000 kg (820,000 lbs) for the equivalent two bays of the Cologne (singly-curved) quadripartite vault. The horizontal thrusts on the primary piers are 28,100 kg (62,000 lbs) and 31,300 kg (69,000 lbs), respectively. The lower horizontal thrust at the secondary pier of the Bourges vault, 11,300 kg (25,000 lbs), however, indicates the inherent potential of the sexpartite, as compared with the quadripartite, vault for covering a large area with a single visual unit of lighter construction and with less total horizontal thrust.[16]

Finally, in comparing the vaulting over two bays, it will be noted that there are two fewer groin ribs in the sexpartite configuration than there are in the equivalent expanse of the quadripartite configuration. Since these ribs weigh nearly 3,600 kg (8,000 lbs) each, their absence helps to explain why the sexpartite vaulting is lighter. It is tempting to suggest that the master who substituted sexpartite vaulting for the original quadripartite choir vaults of Beauvais after the failure of 1284 was well aware of this aspect of the behavior of sexpartite vaults. Indeed, his confidence was such that he provided no additional buttressing to ensure extra lateral bracing for the new secondary pier extensions.

One result of these analyses was the observation that small changes in vault geometry have little effect on overall patterns and magnitudes of vault forces, as is demonstrated by the fact that the results from three different representations of the Cologne geometry were very similar. This is an important observation because it suggests that relatively small differences in vault and bay dimensions in similar buildings, or from one bay to another within a single building, can be expected to produce only relatively small changes with respect to total loadings or thrusts, given the same general vault geometry. This fact helps to explain how a similar vault form might be copied and used successfully in another location. It also indicates that the use of approximations to actual geometry in physical or computer modeling need not inhibit the drawing of general conclusions regarding the structural behavior of vaults.

The second and most important insight concerns the distinctive structural behavior of the quadripartite and sexpartite vault webbing. The webbing clearly acts as three-dimensional structure, and its simplified treatment as a series of almost parallel arches in much of the literature following Abraham has therefore been quite misleading.[17] Major problems in comprehending the structural role of the rib have been caused by this misunderstanding, as was Abraham's own erroneous rolling marble analogy. The fact that the paths of the forces leading to the pier are distributed throughout the webs, as shown by the analysis in this chapter, and are not particularly attracted to the groins indicates the minimal effect of the groin ribs. In the light of this new structural interpretation, the function of the rib in providing centering for the vault during construction and its aesthetic function in covering unsightly joints and guiding the eye upward from the pier shafts, take on an importance greater than any structural function.

NOTES

Material for this chapter was derived from: Robert Mark, John F. Abel, and Kevin O'Neill, "Photoelastic and Finite-element Analysis of a Quadripartite Vault," *Experimental Mechanics* XIII (August 1973):322–329; and from Kurt D. Alexander, Robert Mark, and John F. Abel, "The Structural Behavior of Medieval Ribbed Vaulting," *Journal of the Society of Architectural Historians* XXXVI (December 1977):241–251. For further information on shell structures, see David P. Billington, *Thin Shell Concrete Structures*, 2nd ed. (New York: McGraw-Hill, 1982); and on finite-element analysis, see Chandrakant S. Desai and John F. Abel, *Introduction to the Finite Element Method* (New York: Van Nostrand Reinhold, 1972).

1 Robert Willis, "On the Construction of the Vaults of the Middle Ages," *Transactions of the Royal Institute of British Architects of London*, I, Part ii (1842):3, 24. Willis's study, as he tells us himself in its summary, actually centered on vault geometry and construction, leaving out questions of structural behavior: "Thus, I have said nothing respecting mechanical principles, and have confined myself to form and management. But it appears to me from examination of the works of the Middle Age architects, that the latter considerations had an infinitely greater influence upon their structures than the relations of pressure, then very little understood, and about which they made manifest and sometimes fatal errors."

2 Eugène E. Viollet-le-Duc, *Dictionnaire raisonné de l'architecture française du XIe au XVIe siècle*, 10 vols. (Paris: Librairies-Imprimeries Réunies, 1854–1868), I, pp. 45–46, 73–74, 194; IV, pp. 14, 85, 126; IX, p. 501.

3 Pol Abraham, *Viollet-le-Duc et le Rationalisme Médiéval* (Paris: Vincent, Fréal & Cie., 1934). In all cases, Abraham used the word *thrust* to refer to the horizontal force. For clarity, "horizontal force component" and "horizontal thrust" will be used in the text to indicate horizontal forces within the vault and vault reaction at a support, respectively.

4 Frankl translates this portion of Abraham's passage as follows: "[The marble] does not roll to the wall, of course, but in accordance with the theory that every section parallel to the wall results in a barrel vault which carries itself, along the curve of the section. The marble always rolls in the direction of strongest curvature and, reaching the hollow line above the groin, rolls on in this channel to the pier" (Paul Frankl, *The Gothic: Literary Sources and Interpretations through Eight Centuries* [Princeton: Princeton University Press, 1960], p. 807). Later, in discussing vaults of double curvature (having principal curvature in two orthogonal directions), Abraham pondered the effect of the additional curvature and concluded in the end that the path taken by the marble "will not be essentially different from that described by a cross-sectional cut perpendicular to the axis of the vault." Doubly-curved vaults, he judged, behave in approximately the same manner as vaults of single curvature (Pol Abraham, *Viollet-le-Duc et le Rationalisme Médiéval*, p. 34).

5 It is remarkable that although Abraham notes the presence of diagonal forces along the groins, he does not choose to distinguish their horizontal components, including the horizontal thrust at the piers that requires counteracting flying buttresses.

6 Other arguments included the suggestion that the vaults themselves were too light to need the support of ribs. Furthermore, Abraham asked why the Gothic master made the diagonal ribs less than half the size in cross section of the transverse ribs, which were paradoxically also shorter, if he intended them to bear the major portion of the load? Finally, he pointed to the many instances in which entire sections of ogival ribs had been blown out by bombs in World War I without precipitating the collapse of the vaults above, thereby demonstrating that the use of ribs was often purely decorative.

Abraham also commented on the Gothic builders' approach to construction. He noted that they probably started from simplified assumptions for the intersections of the different sections of a bay and traced them out in plan. Then, he suggested, they could have used a compass to adjust the contours of the ribs to match the lines of intersection. As a result, they would have found it most natural to use the rib primarily as permanent centering and to take advantage of its ability to cover up unsightly gaps and difficult stone work along the lines of intersection (Pol Abraham, *Viollet-le-Duc et le Rationalisme Médiéval*, pp. 38ff.).

7 Paul Frankl, *The Gothic*, p. 810.

8 At Beauvais, it was replaced by sexpartite vaulting after the fall of the quadripartite vaulting in 1284 (see chapter 5).

9 The choir of Cologne, begun in 1248 under the direction of a French-trained master, was not dedicated until 1322. Nevertheless, its design retains enough French High Gothic influence (including height of vaulting, almost matching Beauvais) for it to be counted among the earlier French monuments.

10 Other assumptions and simplifications made for the first model tests were: the vaults were considered uncracked; the vault thickness was kept constant, corresponding to a uniform thickness of 33 cm (13 in) (the actual vault thickness varies from about 25 cm (10 in) at the crown to 50 cm (20 in) near the piers); the loading of the rubble fill at the haunches of the vault was taken into account, but any structural interaction (that is, increased support or stiffening of the vaults) by the fill was omitted; the buttress system supporting the vaults was considered immovable (that is, no translation or rotation was permitted at the vault springing); the model was constructed without ribs; gravity forces were presumed to act only after the vault construction had been completed. In other words, we assumed that rigid centering was used to form the vault and that its removal, allowing vault deformation, had the effect of "turning on" gravity. For details of medieval vault erection, see John Fitchen, *The Construction of Gothic Cathedrals* (Oxford: Clarendon Press, 1961).

11 Techniques for finding directions of stress in photoelastic models of shells are described in Jorge D. Riera and Robert Mark, "The Optical-rotation Effect in Photoelastic Shell Analysis," *Experimental Mechanics* IX (January 1969):9–16.

12 In addition to the vertical and horizontal reactions given in table 2, there is a third, longitudinal horizontal force between the bays. This thrust does not act on a pier, since it is balanced by an opposite thrust of the same magnitude from the adjacent bay. For case 4 (table 2), the prototypical Cologne vault, this thrust was found to be 9,000 kg (20,000 lbs).

13 The computer program used in this analysis was SAP IV, written by E. L. Wilson and K. Bathe at the University of California, Berkeley. The program would have allowed the handling of varying thicknesses of both the vault webbing and the arch ribs (see note 10), but this would have required much additional effort. The assumption of uniform thickness does not greatly affect the overall distribution of forces, but it does change local magnitudes of stress. The program actually produced a higher value for stress in the unribbed 32-cm-thick webs near the point where the vault meets the pier than indicated in the text. The cited value includes analytical compensation for the actual thickness of the web in this region.

14 Robert Branner, *La cathédrale de Bourges et sa place dans l'architecture Gothique* (Paris/Bourges: Éditions Tardy, 1962), insert.

15 See note 10. The bay spacing for Bourges is 13.2 m by 6.6 m (43.3 ft by 21.7 ft). For Cologne it is 13.7 m by 6.9 m (45.0 ft by 22.5 ft). The rise of the vaults of Bourges is 7.0 m (23.0 ft) versus 7.4 m (24.3 ft) for Cologne.

16 Longitudinal horizontal force between the bays at the primary piers is, however, far greater: 19,000 (42,000 lbs) compared with the 9,000-kg (20,000-lb) estimate for quadripartite vaulting (note 12). Indeed, the difficulties presented by having to restrain this greater longitudinal thrust during the construction of the high vaults of High Gothic churches was probably responsible for the adoption of quadripartite vaulting in these buildings.

17 See, for example, Jacques Heyman, *Equilibrium of Shell Structures* (Oxford: Clarendon Press, 1977), pp. 126ff. Heyman's analysis of groined vaults follows that of his earlier publication, "On Rubber Vaults of the Middle Ages and Other Matters," *Gazette des Beaux Arts* LXXI (1968):177–188, which did not benefit from the new, sophisticated modeling techniques described in this chapter.

9

CONCLUSION: THE LEGACY OF GOTHIC STRUCTURE

The progressive reduction of the mass of interior structure in large medieval churches even as they became higher, from the Romanesque, as exemplified by Conques, through the High Gothic, and in certain, later, fourteenth-century churches, makes it clear that experimentation with structure went hand in hand with the more commonly emphasized experimentation in style. This experimentation is illustrated in microscale in table 1 (chapter 7), which lists the slenderness ratios of piers in the main arcades of the major High Gothic churches. Through Reims, Amiens, Cologne, and Beauvais, the most important High Gothic cathedrals following Chartres, there is a gradual increase in pier slenderness ratio, a parameter not directly related to vault height or to any other obvious vessel dimension but certainly indicative of a tendency toward lighter structure.

Nevertheless, the progression was not uniform. A comparison of the pier slenderness ratios of the contemporaneous designs of Chartres and Bourges points to the different approaches to structure taken by their designers and confirms the observation made in chapter 3 that the designer of the choir of Bourges was far more daring than the designer of Chartres. Nor does Palma Cathedral, conceived in a different tradition from the churches of the Île-de-France, follow fully in the general mode; yet the lithe piers of this mid-fourteenth-century building are striking even to the modern eye accustomed to lightweight, contemporary structures. And because the interior of Palma displays exceptional openness for a building of such great size, the cathedral must be taken as a high point in the process of Gothic structural experimentation.

Notwithstanding the many changes in size and form that characterized the process of experimentation in reducing structure, all the elements of the medieval buildings that survive clearly satisfy structural criteria for unreinforced masonry construction: stability against overturning and the prevalence of moderate levels of compression. Three major determinants contributed to this success. First, change in structural design followed a general evolutionary pattern (accompanied by an occasional mutant, such as Bourges). Experience with earlier buildings could, therefore, take the place of some of the information about structural behavior that would be available today through the use in the design process of small-scale physical or numerical computer models.

Second, the elegance of certain structural solutions led me to conclude that the master builders must have been aided by a method of experimental engineering used during construction. This method entailed the observation of tensile cracking in the weak lime mortar between the stones following the removal of temporary centering from buttressing and vaulting. Efforts to avoid further cracking could then have led to refinements in design.

This hypothesis is strengthened by the fact that the superstructure of church buildings was often completed one bay at a time. In these instances, the first bays could have acted as experimental full-scale models to test new ideas and fix the form of succeeding construction. The pinnacles at Amiens, which act as prestressing for the pier buttresses, can be considered an elegant example of this approach.

The "forgiving" nature of typical masonry construction, even with weak mortars, was a third contributing factor. For example, it became apparent from the numerical modeling that small changes in vault geometry did not significantly alter overall structural behavior. Geometry that had proved successful in one building could, therefore, be expected to succeed in another, even if its proportions were slightly altered. It is also known that masonry can withstand some tension (caused by bending) if that tension is confined to a highly localized region. Although the model tests indicated several critical regions where tension was likely to be encountered in Gothic church structure, only one of the buildings studied had actually collapsed under the influence of tensile stress.

The critical regions containing tensile anomalies, which were detected by the model tests, are illustrated in figure 74 and correspond to the following descriptions:

REGION *a*, PIER EXTENSIONS
The considerable wind loads on the high, steep roofs of Gothic churches are transferred to the pier extensions, causing them to bend. This bending contributes to tensile stresses on the windward side of the windward pier extension. These stresses are more critical than stresses in the leeward pier extension because the additional wind-load pressure on the windward parapet is greater than the wind suction on the leeward parapet. Stress in the pier occurs if the loads from the wind are high enough to nullify the compressive stress from the weight of the roof and parapet. At Chartres Cathedral, as described in chapter 3, even with the upper flying buttresses in place, the loading of maximum wind produced appreciable tensile stress in the pier extensions, in spite of their relatively heavy cross section. This bending in the pier buttresses was sometimes ameliorated by raising the height of the rubble surcharge over the vaults, but the surcharge at Chartres was not high enough to be effective.

REGION *b*, PIER EXTENSION–FLYING BUTTRESS JUNCTION
When the buttressing has been misplaced above or below the point at which the pier extension receives the thrust from the vault, and when the rubble surcharge above the haunches of the vault is insufficient to permit the vault's thrust to be transmitted directly to the buttresses, the two offset forces tend to rotate the pier extension. This rotation induces bending in both pier and pier extension. The resul-

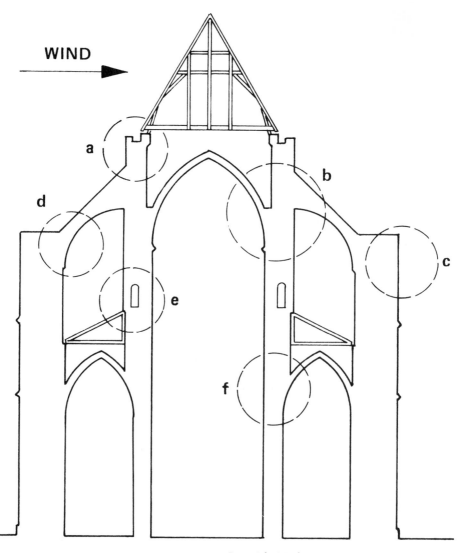

WIND

a

b

d

c

e

f

74 Potential critical-
tension regions in Gothic
construction. These
posed a host of pitfalls for
the buildings' designers
and are of particu-
lar interest to today's
restorers.

tant tensile stresses are usually nullified, as in region *a*, by dead-load compressive stresses. This balance may be upset, however, by the addition of tensile stresses from high wind loading, as in region *c*. The pier extensions may then reveal the effect of tensile stress, as at the church of St. Ouen, Rouen, described in chapter 7.

REGION *c*, PIER BUTTRESSES

The transverse section of a Gothic church can be considered to be a rigid frame. The piers and their extensions, effectively fixed to the foundation by the compressive loads they bear, are connected by a sequence of flying buttresses and vaults. These structures form the cross members of the frame. A rigid frame, acted upon by the lateral loading of the wind, will deform to produce bending in all its members. One result of this bending is a tensile stress on the leeward side of the leeward pier buttress near its top. This tensile stress caused by wind loading may be large enough to nullify the dead-load compressive stresses, which are small because of the small amount of masonry above. The analysis described in chapter 4 shows that at Amiens Cathedral the pinnacles placed on the outside edge of the pier buttresses were sufficient to ensure that tensile stresses produced by high winds would not overcome the combined dead-load compressive stresses.

REGION *d*, FLYING BUTTRESSES

The horizontal members in a rigid frame are also subjected to bending under lateral loads. Since the flying buttresses form cross members in the church's frame, their ends may be expected to develop tensile stresses. Moreover, as the direction of the wind changes from one side of the church to the other, the location of tensile stress will move from the top of the flying buttresses to the bottom, and vice versa. These tensile stresses caused by racking under varying winds will be superimposed on other bending due to the dead load of the flying buttresses.

Though arched construction is ordinarily considered free from dead-load bending, it is reasonable to expect flying buttresses to be subject to some bending because they do not follow a catenary curve and are not uniformly loaded. This is particularly pronounced when the flyers are long and relatively flat, as at Palma Cathedral, described in chapter 7. The bending from the wind and dead loads, which leads to tensile stresses in the flying buttresses, and the exposure of the buttress joints to weathering, necessitate their periodic maintenance in most Gothic construction.

REGION *e*, PASSAGE OPENINGS

Passage openings located in a main structural member may allow forces transmitted by the member to concentrate particularly in the thin web on the outside of the opening. This type of behavior, which can produce local tension and distress, has been observed at the intermediate pier buttresses of the nave of Bourges Cathedral, as discussed in chapter 3.

REGION *f*, INTERSECTION OF PIER AND PIER EXTENSION

The forces that produce bending stresses at the offset intersection of a pier and pier extension resemble those at work in region *b*. In this case, the line of action of the forces acting downward on the pier extension do not directly meet the line of action of the resisting forces in the pier, and the offset produces bending. This bending is not necessarily harmful. For example, the offset shown in figure 74 gives rise to bending in the pier that tends to cancel the bending caused by the thrust of the side aisle vault against it. On one hand, therefore, the effect of the offset can be designed to be beneficial. On the other hand, however, as chapter 5 suggests, tension set up by the offsetting of the intermediate pier buttress at Beauvais Cathedral may have contributed to the collapse of the original high vaults.

With proper attention from building custodial staffs, none of these critical areas should engender serious harm. Indeed, the collapse at Beauvais seems to have come about precisely because this attention was wanting. Moreover, recognizing that the designers of the great Gothic churches were unable to avoid every pitfall awaiting them in no way detracts from the extraordinary feats of High Gothic church construction.

GOTHIC STRUCTURAL RATIONALISM

The results of the model studies indicate that, with regard to the controversy about Gothic form and function, visual impressions aided by superficial analyses can often be misleading. From a purely structural point of view, the studies demonstrate that the vault ribs were not, after all, functional. Once the vault webbing was in place, the ribs played no further *structural* role. Unlike the ribs, which seem functional but are not, the apparently frivolous pinnacles on the pier buttresses of Amiens Cathedral were found to have an important structural function. In the case of the flying buttresses in the classic High Gothic churches, the studies confirmed that these were necessary. However, it became evident that the configuration of the buttress systems was not as efficient as it could have been had their design followed more closely the example of Bourges. An extreme example of poorly designed flying buttresses, in an otherwise elegant structure, is provided by the cathedral of Palma.

As a result of this technical scrutiny, a number of the historical examples cited by Viollet-le-Duc to support his theory of structural rationalism are no longer valid. For instance, as demonstrated in chapter 5 in the case of the overhang of the intermediate piers of Beauvais, Viollet-le-Duc made a rational argument for a detail of design that the model study indicated had contributed to the premature collapse of the building. While Pol Abraham's observations on Gothic structural behavior were generally more astute, they too were largely based on intuition rather than detailed analysis, and as such his inferences are hardly infallible. For instance, his misunderstanding of the function of the pinnacle resulted directly from an oversimplified analysis of its structural action. Abraham properly sensed the ineffectiveness of the vault's ribs, but his argument against the rationality of the rib was primarily based on the role of the natural rib formed by the intersection of the webbing at the groins (figure 64) rather than on the actual distribution of the forces supporting the web which the modeling revealed.

It must be borne in mind, moreover, that the rational argument encompasses a wider sphere than disagreement between Viollet-le-Duc and Abraham over the actual structural performance of Gothic architectural elements. Underlying Viollet-le-Duc's theory are two tacit assumptions: first, the medieval master strove for efficient structure and, second, he perceived the consequences of the decisions he made during the process of design.

With regard to the first assumption, it is sometimes argued that the concept of efficiency, which leads architects to minimize costs by more effective design and by reducing the amount of material needed for a building project, is only a relatively recent manifestation of modern, technological society. It seems more probable, however, that economy of structure was indeed an important consideration during the building of the High Gothic churches. It is inconceivable that such factors as the tremendous cost of obtaining and transporting stone to the building site, or the pressing need to reduce the weight of lofty superstructures to relieve foundation loadings, would not have impelled designers to consider more efficient uses of masonry structure.

With regard to the second assumption, although the Bourges example was not widely followed, indicating that the structural systems of many buildings were not as refined as they could have been, my studies show that the Gothic masters on both sides of the Channel understood well enough the functioning of buttressing. Indeed, the application of pinnacles to pier buttresses to augment cohesion within the masonry indicates a fairly high level of design sophistication. Furthermore, while we do not know for sure how Gothic builders originally viewed the rib, it is possible to infer that it was assumed to strengthen the vaulting, but by 1300, after further experimentation with building, the medieval masters began to perceive its true, nonstructural nature.[1]

It is, therefore, difficult to avoid the conclusion that Viollet-le-Duc's faith in medieval builders was justified and that his interpretation of structural rationalism in Gothic architecture has been largely vindicated.

STRUCTURAL RATIONALISM IN MODERN ARCHITECTURE

Some comments are in order concerning the interpretation of structural rationalism by those who came after Viollet-le-Duc. It has become fashionable today to decry structural rationalism as an architectural ideal. Rationalism is condemned by critics who attribute to it some of the blame for the prevailing sprawl of faceless, glass-walled cityscapes. Yet I perceive that the idea of structural rationalism has rarely been interpreted in its original meaning. To some it is synonymous with Pugin's *True Principles*: "There should be no features about a building which are not necessary for convenience, construction or propriety."[2] Adoption of this view by architects has sometimes distorted the original concept still further by incorporating it into an architectural morality that demands that forms which appear to be structural should act as structure,

even if more efficient alternatives exist. For example, the Sydney Opera House became a vastly extravagant project when it was decided to make its roof shells, which were in no way derived from any structural premise, *honestly* self-supporting. An interior frame, unseen from the halls below, to provide support to the sculptural shells would have made far better engineering sense and would have saved a great deal of money.[3]

For others, rationalism demands the use in architecture of the *symbols* of modern mechanical (or naval) technology, as exemplified by Le Corbusier's forms resembling the upper deck of a ship on the roof of the Unité d'Habitation. A few contemporary designers such as Pier Luigi Nervi, however, have succeeded in developing new styles of architecture according to the principles laid down by Viollet-le-Duc. One of the best examples of Nervi's work is the shell structure of the Small Sports Palace in Rome (figures 8 and 9). Here the building's form is closely related to both its physics and its mode of construction and bears out Nervi's adherence to the *idea* of structural rationalism.[4]

The study of the Gothic vault also provided the mechanism by which to answer the question posed in chapter 1 concerning the logic of employing ribs in a modern thin shell roof. The same computer formulations developed for the earlier study were used to examine modern thin-groined shells made of reinforced concrete, even though these structures are so much thinner and flatter. Analysis of a series of similar, typical modern vaults (a number of which were constructed in the 1950s) yielded some general conclusions that were not unlike those derived from the medieval vault study (compare the force-trajectories of figure 75 with those of figure 67). Indeed the ribs of the modern shells were found to have even less effect on overall structural behavior than the ribs of the medieval vaults. Further it was

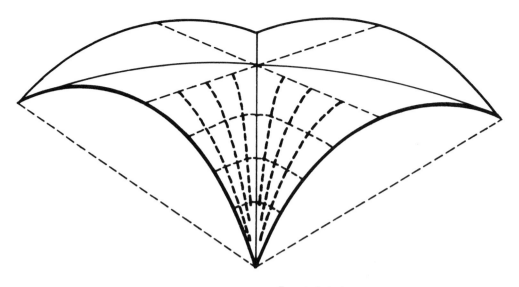

75 Force trajectories
under the action of dead
loads in an intersecting-
barrel, thin shell roof.
Heavy dashed lines indi-
cate the paths of maxi-
mum compression forces.

observed that in modern shell construction, the valley formed at the groin, particularly near the shell supports, would normally be filled with additional reinforced concrete to form a natural rib similar to that found in medieval vaults. The ribs of the St. Louis Airport terminal (figure 10) were consequently ascertained to be generally ineffectual in providing support for uniform gravity loadings. They might, however, play a role in helping to stabilize the shell in the case of non-uniform loadings—by wind or by partial snow coverage—but this would need to be determined from other types of studies which might also employ small-scale models.

Viollet-le-Duc believed that architects should use fully the products of modern technology. His was a positive and forward-looking attitude that refused to enshrine the techniques of the past while acknowledging their brilliance in their own context.

The current study has in its turn taken advantage of technological advances in the analysis of structure to reexamine theories developed when methods of analysis were less sophisticated. The future will doubtless bring further advances in technique, but the use of today's photoelastic and computer-numerical modeling to reexamine Gothic church structure already serves to refine and augment historical scholarship based on primary documents, archaeological evidence, and stylistic analysis. The studies presented here are a beginning. Analysis of groups of buildings from earlier and later epochs, as well as other types of building from the medieval era, will broaden our knowledge of the whole historical development of architecture and design.

Nor is this approach devoid of application to modern structure. As the investigation of the roof of the airport terminal at St. Louis demonstrated, the methods of analysis discussed in this text are capable of providing significant insights into the behavior of contemporary structure and can perhaps enliven a now-neglected field of architectural criticism.

NOTES

1 Paul Frankl dates the beginning of Late Gothic to 1300, when he claims "the function of the rib is ignored." *Gothic Architecture* (Harmondsworth, England: Penguin Books, 1962), p. 146. Near the close of the Gothic era, however, particularly in late English and German churches, there was often a reversal of the roles of the classic vault rib and webbing. Closely spaced ribs in intricate patterns effectively became the actual structure of the vaults with thin webbing acting only to cover the interstices between the ribs.

2 Augustus Welby Pugin, *The True Principles of Pointed or Christian Architecture* (London: John Weale, 1841), p. 1.

3 "When proposed in 1957, officials said the building would cost $9.8 million and be completed in 1964. But almost immediately, the opera house became the victim of its design. . . . The argument over roof design [between architect and engineer] continued over six years during which 350,000 man-hours and 3,000 computer hours were consumed. The final cost of the project exceeded the original estimate by $132 million" (*Engineering News Record*, April 5, 1973, p. 13).

4 Pier Luigi Nervi's philosophy of design is set out in his *Structures*, translated by G. and M. Salvadori (New York: McGraw-Hill, 1956).

APPENDIX: SOME DEFINITIONS

While an effort has been made to minimize jargon in the text, the nature of the subject demands that some technical terms be used. This appendix, intended to acquaint the nonspecialist reader with their meaning, has two parts. The first deals with engineering terminology, with the order of the terms selected to form a coherent explanation of the basic behavior of structures. The second part, comprising architectural terms, is ordered alphabetically.

ENGINEERING TERMS

structural loadings Loadings are classified as dead and live. *Dead* loadings do not change over time and include the self-weight of the fixed structure of a building. *Live* loadings vary with time; such loadings include the weight of people and furniture in the interior of a building and of wind and snow acting on its exterior.

forces For a structure to maintain its integrity (equilibrium) when loadings are applied to it, resisting forces within the structure must counteract the loadings. For example, if a cable is used in a hoist to lift a weight, the cable will be subjected to *tensile* (stretching) force equal to the weight lifted. If a stone is placed on end as in figure *a,* it undergoes *compression* from its own weight. At the top of the stone the compression force is zero; at its base the force is equal to the total weight of the stone. If the upright stone is loaded by an additional, concentrically placed weight, as in figure *b,* the compression force is increased by the magnitude of the weight: at the top of the stone, the compression force is equal to the applied weight, and at its base, the compression force is equal to the weight of the stone plus the applied weight.

If the stone is now placed on its side and supported only at its ends, as in figure *c,* the weight of the stone will subject it to *bending* forces. With bending, the lower portion of the stone will stretch, indicat-

ing that tension is present—"t" denotes
this tensile region, and "c" the accom-
panying compression region at the top of
this beamlike structure. The horizontal
stone is subjected also to *shear* forces.
One could imagine that if the stone was
instead composed of soft butter, its
supports might slice off its ends. These
slicing, shearing forces exist also in
the stone, but in this particular illustration, they are of but slight magnitude.

In most structures, a combination
of these forces is required for equilibrium.
The upright stone illustrated in figure *d*
is undergoing not only compression from
its own weight and an external load but
also bending from the eccentric application
of the external load. If the external load
and its eccentricity are sufficiently large,
the stone will experience tension in the
region indicated by *t*. Figure *e* illustrates
a voussoir acting essentially in compression, as in figures *a* and *b*, but with
a small amount of bending from both its
own weight, as in figure *c*, and from
eccentricity of the forces acting on it from
the adjacent voussoirs as in figure *d*.

resolution of forces into components It is
often convenient to resolve inclined forces,
such as the compression force acting on
the voussoir (*e*), into vertical and horizontal components, that is, to replace it by
two imaginary forces that have the same
structural effect as the single inclined
force. This is done geometrically: if the
length of line F represents the magnitude
and direction of the inclined force, the
lengths of the vertical (V) and horizontal
(H) legs of the right triangle formed
with (F) as hypotenuse give the magnitudes
of these components.

reactions These are the forces that
occur in a loaded structure at its support(s).
For example, in figure *a*, the reaction at
the base of the stone is a vertical compression force equal to the weight of the stone.
In figure *d*, the reaction at the base consists of a compressive force equal to

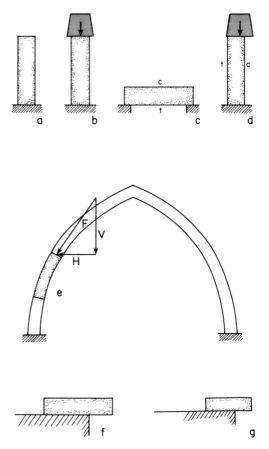

Structural modes.

the weight of the stone plus the applied weight and a bending force proportional to the applied weight and its eccentricity.

The *conditions of support* greatly affect the actual reactions. For example, the base supports are shown to provide *fixity* (against translation and rotation) for all the illustrated stones. If the stone of figure *d* was supported only by a *hinge* attachment against vertical force, it would prove unstable, and a second point of reaction would be needed to maintain equilibrium.

deformations Deformation is exhibited by all materials subjected to loading. Compression causes shortening, tension causes lengthening, and bending produces curvature. In most engineering structures deformation is not directly observable, yet it can be measured with sensitive instrumentation. The *stiffness* of a structure, a measure of its tendency to deform, is determined by considering its overall configuration and the materials of its construction. Under ordinary loading conditions, building materials can be considered *elastic*; that is, when the loading is removed, they return, as does deformed elastic-rubber, to their original form. Very high loadings and loadings of very long duration can, however, produce additional permanent deformation known as *creep*.

stress Stress is a measure of the local intensity of force acting within a structure. For a simple concentrically loaded strut, the stress is found merely by dividing the total force carried by the strut by its cross-sectional area. For example, if a strut of 5 cm² (0.77 sq in) cross section is compressed by a 10-kg (22-lb) force, the *compressive stress* within the strut is 10 kg/5 cm² = 2 kg/cm² (28.4 psi). In the same manner, tension forces give rise to *tensile stress* and shear forces to *shear stress*. Bending, which is normally accompanied by tension, compression, and shear forces, can give rise to all three types of stress.

stress analysis As the loading, configuration, and support conditions of structures become more intricate, finding the distribution of local forces and stresses within them is all the more complex. Engineers have developed analytical stress solutions for many types of structural configuration, but these are usually limited to structures having well defined, regular geometries and loadings. *Structural modeling* is used to solve for the force and stress distributions within the more intricate structural configurations. One approach is *physical modeling*, in which measurements are made on small-scale models of the structure; one of the most powerful physical modeling techniques, based on the interference patterns produced in polarized light by stressed transparent model materials, is photoelasticity. A second approach is *numerical modeling*, in which the abstracted material properties, geometry, and loading of the structure are set out in an electronic computer to produce information on deformation, forces, and stresses.

strain Strain is a measure of local deformation within a structure. *Tension, compression*, and *shear strains* generally accompany tension, compression, and shear stresses. If the physical properties of the structure are established and the stress is determined from a stress analysis, the strain is easily found. Conversely, if the physical properties are established and the strains are known, stresses are easily calculated. Hence *electric strain gauges*, which precisely measure strain in a full-scale structure or a small-scale model, can also be used to determine stresses.

strength The strength of a material is defined as the stress level that causes the material to fail. When the stress within a structure exceeds the material's strength, structural damage occurs. For most engineering materials, compression (crushing) strengths are higher than tension (tearing) strengths; for example, the tensile strength of masonry is usually an order of magnitude less than its compressive strength.

stability Structural instability is a second mode of failure, unrelated to the strength of a structure (unless the breaking of a structural element is the cause of the instability). The general principle of stability is illustrated in figure *f*. With the stone's *center of gravity* (the point within the stone where its weight may be considered to act) placed within the boundary of the surface below it, the stone will remain safely on the surface—it is stable. If the stone is moved outward so that its center of gravity falls outside the boundary of the surface, the stone will rotate and fall—it becomes unstable. The Gothic pier buttress provides another example of possible instability. The thrust of a flying buttress near the top of a pier buttress tends to overturn it. If the mass and base dimensions of the pier buttress are insufficient, this structure could fail through overturning instability, even if its strength is sufficient to maintain its integrity under the loading of the flying buttress.

Another mode of instability can occur in a strut or a pier even though its material strength is far greater than the nominal value of compressive stress (found by dividing the compressive force within the member by its cross-sectional area). Because such a member is slender and often not exactly true in all its dimensions, accidental bending stresses will accompany the nominal compressive stress, and the total of both types of stress can induce a mode of failure known as *column buckling*. Avoiding this phenomenon is an important design consideration in slender structures

of metal and reinforced concrete, but it is only rarely encountered in more massive masonry construction.

modeling similitude Some principles of similitude are illustrated by comparing figures *f* and *g*. If the small-scale *model* *g* is placed on the supporting surface in exact relation to the larger *prototype f*, it too will be stable, even if it is made from a different and lighter (or heavier) material. Likewise, if the small-scale model is placed so that its center of gravity falls outside the supporting surface, it will be unstable. Hence the small-scale model could be used to predict the instability of the prototype. This same principle would have allowed the medieval builder to construct a model of his building at very small scale (with each stone represented) even of wood if he chose, to predict the stability of the masonry prototype under the effect of gravity loadings. However, the magnitude of stresses between the stones and their supports in figures *f* and *g* is not the same. This is because the volume of the stone, and hence its weight, increases with the cube of its scale while the area of contact between the stone and its support increases only as the square of its scale. The larger stone experiences higher stresses. Hence *scaling laws*, which can relate the stresses in a model to the stresses in a prototype, would need to be applied before the model could be used to predict strength, and it is highly unlikely that these laws were known to medieval builders.

ARCHITECTURAL TERMS

ambulatory Aisle around the eastern end of a church.

apse Semicircular or polygonal termination of the eastern end of the church.

ashlar Square-hewn, dressed stone; also, masonry in which all stones are squared, giving a uniform pattern of vertical and horizontal joints.

bay Compartments into which a building is divided, normally marked by its piers.

beam Generally, a long structural member carrying loadings that are transverse to its longitudinal axis and which produce shearing and bending forces.

buttress Mass of masonry attached to a wall to help it to resist lateral, overturning forces. A *flying buttress* is an archlike structure that normally acts as a compression brace against lateral forces.

capital The transitional block between the pier and upper wall.

catenary The shape assumed by a hanging chain under the action of gravity. The curve of a catenary is very close to that of a parabola.

centering Temporary shoring, usually constructed of timber, to support vaulting or flying buttresses during their construction.

choir The portion of a church where services are sung—generally at its eastern end.

clerestory The wall, or story, that rises above the aisle roof, usually pierced by large windows in Gothic churches.

colonnette A light (vertical) column not usually part of the primary building structure.

course A line of stone blocks. *Coursed* masonry is composed of lines of blocks, but it may contain *broken courses* when the joints are not all in the same plane.

crossing The space formed by the central piers at the intersection of the longitudinal and lateral axes in a cruciform-plan church.

footing The projecting base of a pier or a wall that distributes loadings to a wider area of subsoil.

frame A structural assembly of beamlike elements, generally formed of timber in medieval construction, and of steel or reinforced concrete in large-scale, modern construction.

hemicycle The semicircular structure of the rounded termination of a church.

nave The main portion or central aisle of the church, generally at its western end and devoted to the lay worshipper.

pier An upright structure of masonry acting mainly to support vertically acting loads.

pier buttress The massive, upright structures along the perimeter of the church that provide support to the outer ends of the flying buttresses. *Intermediate pier buttresses* are the lighter uprights often used to support the center of the flying buttress system in churches with five aisles.

pier extension The skeletal upright structure that extends above the pier into the clerestory and forms, with the pier, the major vertical structural element of a Gothic church.

string course A continuous horizontal molding or projection across the surface of a wall.

strut A light, slender structural member subjected to compressive forces along its longitudinal axis.

template A pattern used to establish the profile of cut stone—used also to profile photoelastic models.

tie beam The lowest main horizontal member of a roof truss that acts in tension to prevent the roof framing from spreading. It does not actually function primarily as a beam.

transept The transverse arms of a church of cruciform plan, usually forming a separation between the choir and the nave.

triforium The wall passage above the arcade story and below the clerestory in mature Gothic churches.

truss A skeletal, structural assembly of struts and beamlike elements generally used to carry loadings applied transverse to its horizontal axis. For example, see the timber roof truss of Reims Cathedral illustrated in figure 1.

vault A masonry structure of arched section, forming a ceiling or roof. A *barrel vault* is a continuous vault of semicircular section. *Groined vaults* are formed by intersecting two orthogonal barrel vaults, the *groins* being the lines of intersection. *Quadripartite vaulting* divides each bay of vaulting into four compartments, as illustrated in plate 7. *Sexpartite vaulting* divides each pair of bays into six compartments, as illustrated in plate 8. *Ribs* are the stone arches projecting below the vaulting surface and thought to provide permanent centering. The *webbing* is the stone surface of a vault seen as infilling between the ribs. *Surcharge* is a concrete mass composed of rubble and mortar placed over the haunches of the vault.

voussoir Wedge-shaped stone used as the building block of an arch or a vault.

INDEX